Numbers in the Newsroom

USING MATH AND STATISTICS IN NEWS
SECOND EDITION

By Sarah Cohen

Investigative Reporters & Editors, Inc.

Editor:
Dan Claxton

Design:
Wendy Gray

ISBN 0-9766037-1-3

One in an ongoing series of beat books and reporting guides
by Investigative Reporters & Editors, Inc.

Please direct comments and suggested updates to:
beatbooks@ire.org.

Foreward

This guide would not have been possible without advice and help from many corners. The original version was informed by practioners Neill Borowski then of The Philadelphia Inquirer, Dan Browning of the Minneapolis Star-Tribune, Ron Campbell of the Orange County Register, Chris Callahan now dean of Arizona State University's journalism school, Jo Craven McGinty of The Wall Street Journal, Stephen Doig of Arizona State University, Ford Fessenden of The New York Times, Dan Keating of The Washington Post, Jennifer LaFleur of the Center for Investigative Reporting, Andy Lehren of The New York Times, Philip Meyer of the University of North Carolina and Patrick Remington of the University of Wisconsin. Over the years, we've received input from many more corners.

Thanks to all of those who helped focus this handbook and provide suggestions. Thanks also to Wendy Gray for graphics assistance and design, Lauren Grandestaff for editing and Zana Lo of IRE for seeking additional resources for reporters.

If you just want an overview of the concepts in this book, feel free to watch the video created for Columbia Journalism School's Stabile program for a Spring 2014 class at https://www.youtube.com/watch?v=lZjsCycecNc

And special thanks to Len Bruzzese, and Brant Houston at IRE for shepherding this original project, and Dan Claxton and Mark Horvit for this newer effort.

TABLE OF CONTENTS

INTRODUCTION

Introduction

"Statistics are people with the tears washed off "

– Paul Brodeur

For two years, as training director for Investigative Reporters & Editors, I tried to help reporters, editors and producers overcome their terror of numbers. It's less fun than pressing buttons on a keyboard. But these journalists understood the need to feel more comfortable with the numbers they see every day if they're ever going to bring their reporting and even their writing to a new level.

This guide takes an approach that I hope will give you a few simple ways to describe the living world that numbers represent. It's based on the idea that you'll find implied in books on the topic of innumeracy, statistics and graphics. That is, selecting the right number for just the right place in a story depends on the same news judgment you use in selecting just the right quote, anecdote or image.

It's our job to put everything we learn into perspective in a story, not just the words or pictures. I hope whether you read this all the way through or use it as a deadline guide, you'll come away with more confidence to select or compute the numbers you need for your story.

In the decade since that original version, we've seen the use of data in news transformed from a simple chart in the newspaper to dazzling interactive displays. The data journalism movement has helped push journalists toward being more comfortable with statistics and data.

So is there really a need for another tome on this topic? I think the answer is still "yes."

Some others lead to paralysis. They lecture reporters on our inability to adequately understand or balance every number we publish. No number is perfect. So some critics deride them all, picking out examples of improper uses of numbers as if there were a correct answer for every story. In the end, they often leave us with the impression that we can't use any numbers without fearing retribution.

Still other guides focus on statistical issues that arise less often in the newsroom: probability, sampling and survey design. Yes, we report on studies that have used these methods, and I've provided a brief checklist for people who need to know more.

But if your job involves regularly reporting on research or surveys, as in medical reporting or politics, I suggest you pick up one of the excellent books available for the newsroom. Both "News and Numbers," by Victor Cohn, and "The Newsroom Guide to Polls and Surveys," are useful. I won't repeat what those authors have done.

CHAPTER 1:
What's a Number?

We often ask too much of numbers, and that's why we're uncomfortable with them.

A number is an opinion. It's just hidden behind scientific-sounding methods and carries an air of authority. Some opinions carry the credibility of years of impartial study. Others don't.

A number is a summary. Some numbers help paint accurate portraits of the living, breathing world the number represents. Others don't.

A number is a guess. The 2000 U.S. presidential election, which hinged on a few dozen voters in Florida, reminded us that even something as simple as a vote tally may be inaccurate. Some guesses are close enough to use without warning. Others aren't.

Keeping these views of numbers in mind will help you avoid the so-called lies that numbers are accused of spreading. And putting numbers in their place – using them as opinions, as summaries and as guesses – is one way to reduce the mind-numbing accumulation of numbers in a story.

SEVEN TIPS TO KEEP YOUR COPY NUMBER-FREE AND FAIR

Once, there was broad acceptance in newsrooms that reporters – and their editors – can't handle math. It was a badge of honor, perhaps marking the writer as an accomplished wordsmith or observer of the human condition. No more. It's no longer considered cute. Now, the fear of numbers marks a reporter as one who can only do part of the job. Reporters who give into that fear will have difficulty reporting on a complex story if they can't overcome it. But how? Here are some simple tips to tame numbers and help you improve stories that depends on them.

1. KEEP THE NUMBER OF DIGITS IN A PARAGRAPH BELOW EIGHT

Reducing the number of numbers in our copy can actually improve how we use the ones we're allocated. One suggestion, adapted from others, is to reduce the number of digits in a paragraph to eight.

Don't cheat by stacking paragraphs with eight digits on top of one another. Separate any number-packed paragraphs with anecdotes, sources' explanations, quotes or observations before you allow yourself more numbers.

This exercise, borrowed from William Blundell's Art and Craft of Feature Writing is geared at forcing you to choose your numbers as carefully as you choose your quotes. It also forces you to find simpler ways to describe the numbers using words like "double" or "nearly" or "more than." And it forces you to demand that your sources simplify their numbers enough for you to summarize them.

Why eight? This usually gives you the ability to fit one year and two substantive numbers into a paragraph. Look for a way, though, to reduce this number of digits by simplifying to stress the most important point.

Here's an updated version of Blundell's example. You'd be over your allocation with a sentence like this:

> The Office of Redundancy's budget rose 48 percent in 2013, from $700.3 million to $1.03 billion.

Think about how it could change:

> Over the past year, the Office of Redundancy's budget grew by nearly half, to $1 billion.

If you follow this exercise, you'll find your copy reads more smoothly and conveys more meaning. You also may find yourself working more closely with the copy desk and your graphics department, using the space you save to convey information more effectively through graphics.

2. MEMORIZE SOME COMMON NUMBERS ON YOUR BEAT

The hardest part of dealing with numbers is answering the question, "Is it big or is it small?"

You can start to answer this question by memorizing some common numbers on your beat and keeping them in mind as you report.

For instance, U.S. reporters have to know its population (about 317 million at this writing), the size of its economy (estimated at $16.2 trillion in 2012) and the income of the typical household in the country (about $51,000).

Each beat also has its own specialized numbers.

In education, they might include teacher salaries, the budget of the school district and the pass rate of students in the top and bottom performing schools. In medical reporting, you might need to know the annual number of deaths each year in the U.S., the number of smokers or the leading causes of death. And in government reporting, the typical campaign war chest and the local budget are crucial.

John Allen Paulos calls this "building a sense of scale." You can call it knowing the difference between a big number and a small number. It gives you the all-important "compared to what?" in a story. If nothing else, it reduces errors.

For instance, an editor reduced Wal-Mart's sales from $1.2 billion to $1.2 million over the weekend without calling the reporter. She later said she thought "billion" sounded too big. This was a case of failing to understand scale in retailing. If she'd known that $1 billion in sales wasn't particularly large, or that Wal-Mart had sales of 100 times that amount when this mistake occurred In the 1990s, she'd have never made the mistake.

How can you memorize these numbers? It's not so hard, and you don't have to pull out an almanac and start memorizing. Just start by paying attention to the numbers you have to look up all the time. Try guessing before you look it up. It might cement the right answer in your head.

3. ROUND OFF – A LOT

Notice the numbers quoted so far: They're far from exact.

In fact, you can afford to be less exact early in your reporting. You'll need the most precise number before you characterize it in your story. But "characterize" is the important word here. Philip Meyer, in Precision Journalism said it this way: "Decimal points are for meaning, not emphasis." Only use extra precision when it matters.

In fact, while reporting, it would be perfectly respectable for you to know that the population in the U.S. is more than 300 million. That's close enough to evaluate whether any other number is big or small. It also makes it easier to do some figures in your head.

This exercise reduces your dependence on exact numbers. It reduces the hair-splitting that many people find themselves in when dealing with numbers that don't deserve it. It also stops you from focusing on meaningless differences.

4. LEARN TO THINK IN RATIOS

Most of the math we use in the newsroom revolves around ratios of some kind: A percentage, a percentage difference, a rate or a value per person.

The reason is that we can't think clearly about very big or very small numbers. For example, you can picture the number 5. It might be fingers or toes, it might be a Supreme Court majority, or it might be the number of runs scored in a baseball game. But change it to 355, and the picture gets fuzzier. Maybe it's a movie theater. Change that to 317 million, and you can't picture it at all. The same thing happens when numbers get really small. Once you've gone below about one-quarter, you will have a hard time picturing what it means.

So make the numbers you deal with understandable by learning to think in simple ratios.

Let's take an example: The estimates of fixing the Year 2000 computer bug. A widely quoted estimate was $50 billion for U.S. companies. How big is $50 billion? At the time, it was smaller than Bill Gates' net worth. It was the cost of two hurricanes. It was the income of people living in the Portland, Ore., area.

This isn't to say that the problem wasn't newsworthy. The possible widespread effect and the uncertainty surrounding it made the problem significant and newsworthy. But it wasn't a financial disaster.

5. USE DEVICES FROM EVERYDAY LIFE

Sports fans have an advantage when it comes to working with numbers. Basketball players think in terms of "1 for 10" or "2 for 8." Baseball fans already know how to calculate a rate – either an earned run average or a batting average.

But even if you're not a sports fan, you usually have some arithmetic you perform instinctively. You might figure out how many hours until deadline, or how much a $20 item ought to cost if it's offered during a 10 percent off sale.

If you shop on sale, invest in your retirement, follow sports closely or tip at a restaurant, you know how to do most of the math that we use in daily reporting. Simply convert your reporting questions into this scale.

For example, if you know that Hispanics make up more than 15 percent of the U.S. population, it doesn't take too much work to figure out how many people that is. It's like figuring a small tip on a restaurant bill.

6. ENVISION YOUR DREAM NUMBER AND CALCULATE IT IF IT ISN'T GIVEN TO YOU

Journalist Drew Sullivan recommends that reporters "envision success" when struggling through one of the hardest parts of computer-assisted reporting. This trick works when you're away from the computer, too.

Write your sentence, leaving out the key number. It helps if you have some clue what that number would be – 10 percent or 90 percent, $2 or $300,000. Now track down or calculate the number you need to fill in the holes.

You may find that the numbers don't support your preconceptions. Or you may find that the numbers you've been given so far don't answer any question you care about. That's frustrating. We all, at times, want to dump our notebooks onto the page. But it will help you figure out what's missing early enough to do something about it.

7. LEARN FROM ONE ANOTHER

We all have different strengths.

Visual journalists and broadcasters instinctively understand their viewers' inability to focus on too many numbers at once. Narrative reporters often work well with their graphics departments and web developers to remove important numbers from copy and put them into charts. Take advantage of the specialties in your newsroom or your colleagues in a different medium. Ask for help if you are working on your own by seeking out experts in different specialties, including other IRE members.

GOOD HABITS FOR REPORTING WITH NUMBERS

Part of our fear of numbers comes from the good habits required to avoid embarrassing corrections and mis-pitched stories. These habits are boring. But if you get used to them, you'll often find yourself working quicker at the end of a story.

USE THE TOOLS AVAILABLE TO YOU

There are tools to help us with arithmetic. Use them. All of the common computer operating systems come with a calculator

If you learn a little about spreadsheets, you'll find it's a particularly powerful calculator that repeats your formulas over and over with a single mouse click. That's good.

As Ronald Campbell, who taught math to journalists at The Orange County Register says, you were never good at it anyway. So use the help that's available.

CHECK YOUR ANSWERS, THEN CHECK THEM AGAIN.

Whenever you do take out a calculator, be prepared to compute each answer at least twice. Not enough reporters do this.

You should do it. Always do it. And if you don't have time to do it, don't calculate any numbers.

For spreadsheet users, be prepared to manually spot check your formulas, double-check any numbers you type, and confirm simple summary measures with any totals you can find and the raw numbers from a printed report.

Some reporters print out a draft of the story, then circle every number (and every name) in it and double-check it. This includes years, numbers given to you by a source and numbers you calculate yourself. Try it. It might frighten you into good habits when you discover how often mistakes are buried in your copy.

Although it's not always possible, it helps if you can work with another reporter, a copy editor or someone else you trust during the math phase of your reporting.

ASK YOURSELF IF THE ANSWER MAKES SENSE

Always force a gut-check on your numbers. Use them in a couple of sentences. Ask yourself whether you'd believe them if a fellow journalist (rather than a math-savvy expert) gave them to you.

If you can't figure out if you believe them, then it's time to go back to some of the other tips in this book – working out ratios, rounding off, or looking up some general numbers on the topic.

In a letter to The Washington Post in October 1998, a reader challenged an op-ed piece describing the Census Bureau's plans to estimate information for 27 million people in 78,000 households. The letter writer surmised something was wrong with the published numbers. The reader was right. Such an estimate would lead to almost 350 people in each of the affected households.

Some numbers, like this one, simply don't stand up to common sense. If yours don't, make sure you haven't misunderstood the calculation, mistyped the numbers, or misread the results.

CHAPTER 2:
A Newsroom Math Guide

Virtually every number we use must be compared with something – another time, another place or a total. This newsroom math guide helps you put numbers into perspective using three devices: "Per" something, change, and averages.

These are simple arithmetic problems – formulas many of us learned sometime around fourth grade. Unfortunately, we had another decade to forget them before we got into reporting – then got caught in the trap of math phobia – before these simple tools became second nature.

The good news is that most news stories don't depend on fancy math. Master this arithmetic again, and you'll be able to tackle most reporting jobs.

THE PERS: FRACTIONS, RATES, PERCENTS AND PER CAPITA

You can usually simplify your story if you can re-jigger your numbers into a rate, a ratio or a percentage. "One out of four" is a fraction, or a rate. "Forty percent" is another ratio or rate. And 235 deaths per 100,000 people is another.

Percents and fractions are used to reduce the scale of very large numbers while putting them into perspective.

Rates are also used to level the playing field – they compare two items that have a different base. They can put very small numbers into perspective as well.

When you see a lot of numbers in copy, examine them to see if a simple rate – "one of four" or 25 percent – would simplify your story.

FRACTIONS AND PERCENTS

Repeat this: "Percents are fractions. Fractions are percents."

Remembering this all the time will keep you focused on the key element of percentages: They're ratios, or rates, expressed as a fraction of 100.

Cutting it into two words helps: per (or "for every") cent (or 100, like in "century"). So 25 percent means 25 out of every 100 people, dollars, cars or anything else.

Fractions are easier on readers and viewers than percentages, so use them when they're simpler.

FIGURING A PERCENT:	Step 1: Know your base. Think of the words "out of." It's the total of all the groups.
	Step 2: Divide the category you care about by the base. Remember that a fraction sign (/) means "divided by" (÷).
	Step 3: Move the decimal point two places to the right (or multiply by 100) to get the rate per hundred, or percent.
	Step 4: Round the answer to no more than one decimal place. Better yet, look for an easier fraction your readers will understand.
FORMULA:	Step 1: Total = The base
	Step 2: (Category / Total) = Proportion or rate
	Step 3: Proportion x 100 = Percent
	Step 4: Percent rounded

EXAMPLE:	If 58 people say they will vote in an upcoming election and 92 say they won't, here's how to figure out the percent of people who say they will vote:
	Step 1: Base = number of people asked = 92 + 58 = 150
	Step 2: Rate = 58 out of 150 = 58/150 = .386666..
	Step 3: Percent = .38666... x 100 = 38.666666....
	Step 4: Round and simplify: = 38.7 percent, or more than a third.

FROM FRACTIONS TO PERCENTS AND BACK AGAIN

In a story, it's much easier to understand a simple fraction than a precise percent. so get used to converting fractions to percentages and back.

You know that one out of four is one-quarter, and that it's also 25 percent. but you may not know how to get from one to another.

FROM FRACTIONS TO PERCENTS:
1/4 = 1 ÷ 4 = 0.25. move the decimal place over two places, or multiply by 100, to get 25%

FROM PERCENTS TO FRACTIONS:
In the resources chapter of this book is a list of common fractions and their translations into percentages for more complex numbers. but if you want to calculate them yourself, here's how:

1. Write your percent as a fraction: 25/100

2. Try to find a "least common denominator:" 25 in this case goes into both the top and the bottom. you might want to round off either number to come out to a simple denominator.

3. Simplify: (25 / 25) / (100 / 25) = 1 / 4

TO GET "ONE OUT OF " NUMBERS:

1. Divide your percentage by 100, so 25% is 0.25.

2. Now divide one by that number: 1 / .25 = 4, so your answer is one-fourth.

Tip for spreadsheet users: Excel allows you to format a number as a fraction or a percent. play around with formats to see how the number is most easily described.

PER PERSON (OR PER CAPITA): DEATH RATES, CRIME RATES AND OTHER RATES

As with percentages, per person or per capita rates are used to level the playing field.

They're often used when you need to compare two dissimilar places or events: Crimes in cities with different populations, deaths from various diseases or Gross Domestic Product across countries.

Rates also are often used with very big or very small numbers to change them into something we can understand.

It's difficult to understand very large numbers. In fact, "million" sounds a lot like "billion." But, as John Allen Paulos notes in "Innumeracy," a million seconds go by in 11 days. It would take about 32 years to reach a billion seconds.

Very small numbers produce the same amount of confusion: .003 looks a lot like 0.3. Both are difficult to picture.

RATES FOR LARGE NUMBERS –

PER-PERSON AVERAGES

A raw per-person figure is an average and should usually be used with very big numbers.

A Gross Domestic Product of $17 trillion is hard to digest. So we reduce it to a number we can understand. If we divide it by 317 million, we get about $54,000 for every man, woman and child in the country. It doesn't mean that each person earns $54,000 in fact, almost half of all families earn less than that altogether.

Instead, it includes all of the wealth that is generated and kept by companies as well as people.

But the device turns an incomprehensible number into something we can picture. It also helps if we want to compare countries, for instance – it levels the playing field by adjusting for the size of the country.

RATES FOR SMALL NUMBERS – CRIME, DEATH AND OTHER RARE EVENTS

Other rates – "per 1,000 people" or something like it – are the same as percentages, but you multiply by something bigger than 100 or move the decimal place further to the right. Use these for very small numbers.

If 2.5 million people die in this country every year, then the percentage of people who die is a really small number: 0.789 percent or 0.00789 as a proportion.

A number that little is hard to digest. So experts up the ante and express the figure as 789 deaths per 100,000 people.

FIGURING A RATE:	Step 1: Choose your base. This is often difficult. In reporting on fatalities by make of car, should you use the number of cars on the road, the number sold, or the total miles driven each year? You'll have to decide.
	Step 2: Divide the number you care about by the base. Choosing the numerator can also be tricky. Going back to the automobile fatality example, would you use the total number of deaths or the number of driver deaths? Take a hint using other reports you see on the topic. Experts have often come to an informal agreement about what the most telling number is.
	Step 3: Multiply by a nice round number, such as 1,000, 100,000 or 1 million.
	Step 4: Round the answer and simplify.
FORMULA:	Step 1: Choose the base, or "total"
	Step 2: (Category / Total) = Proportion or Rate
	Step 3: Proportion x 1,000 = Rate per thousand
	Step 4: Round to zero decimal places

EXAMPLE: According to the FBI Crime in the United States for 2012, there were 13,000 violent and property crimes in Pittsburgh out of a population of 312,000. There were 8,870 crimes in tucson out of a population of 531,000. Figuring a rate per thousand residents lets you compare the two cities:

PITTSBURGH

Step 1: base = 312,000 people

Step 2: 13,000 crimes / 312,000 people = .041

Step 3: 0.041 X 1,000 = 41 crimes per 1,000 people

TUCSON

Step 1: base = 531,000 people

Step 2: 8,870 / 531,000 people = 0.017

Step 3: .017 X 1,000 = 17 crimes per 1,000 people

So the crime rate for Pittsburgh is nearly than 2 1/2 times that of tucson – 41/ 17 = 2.4

SELECTING YOUR MULTIPLIER

Some people feel that changing their multiplier from 100 to something bigger is cheating.

After all, a 0.2 percent rate becomes a big number – 200 – when you change the base from 100 to 100,000!

In practice, though, there's nothing magical about using a base of 100 (or percent). Instead, use the number that makes sense for the comparison you're making.

a) Choose a round number – 1,000, 1 million or 100,000.

b) Choose the same number that the experts use: Crimes per 1,000 people, or deaths per 100,000, for instance.

c) Choose a base that will give you an easy way to express it to your readers. This is one that results in a number generally between 1 and 1,000 or so.

d) Try to avoid using an outrageously large base. For instance, avoid expressing a local number in terms of 1 million people. Only a handful of cities have more than a million people.

e) Keep the same base throughout your story. Don't shift from 100,000 to 1,000 in crime statistics, for instance, when you move from murders to total crime rates.

You'll often have to balance these rules of thumb against one another to come up with a good compromise.

GOING FURTHER WITH THE PERS: DOING MATH WITH RATES

You can probably get by in a newsroom without ever learning any more on percents, rates and fractions than what you got in the last section. But many of us have found ourselves with the need to do math with rates – a tricky operation that you have to think about twice before moving on.

ADDING AND SUBTRACTING RATES

If you want to add rates or percentages together, they must come from the same base. That is, you have to have the same "out of" words in each rate before you can add or subtract them to come up with anything of meaning. It's usually used for combining small categories into a catch-all, or in expressing election returns.

The answer to adding and subtracting rates is expressed as percentage points, not percentage: In the popular vote, Barack Obama got 4 percentage points more than Mitt Romney in 2012.

RATES OF RATES, OR "RELATIVE RISK"

As in the crime example, the most powerful kind of ratio is sometimes the one that compares two rates to each other.

Comparing two rates is how we can say, "Black applicants are denied mortgages at twice the rate of whites with similar incomes."

This is called "relative risk."

That term comes from medical research: The risk of contracting a disease among smokers versus non-smokers. We've been taught for so long that we're never allowed to take a rate of a rate that we often cringe at it. But there's nothing illegitimate about it, and relative risk often produces the exact picture we need.

Note, though, that a relative risk isn't reversible. It's easiest to see with small numbers. If 20 smokers per thousand contracted cancer, and the rate was only 10 for non-smokers, the relative risk of smoking is 2 – you're twice as likely to contract cancer as a smoker than as a non-smoker. But someone who doesn't smoke has half the chance, not 200 percent less chance, of developing the disease.

Choose the direction of the relative risk based on the group "at risk."

Also watch your language on these numbers. A smoker has twice the risk, not a two times higher risk, of contracting cancer. If you want to talk about "more than," or "less than," then you have to compute a percent difference between smokers and non-smokers, which involves another step.

As a rule of thumb, rare events generate very large relative risks. So in medical reporting, it's customary to focus only on rates that generate relative risks bigger than double or triple. But for larger numbers – or more common events, such as the chances of getting a mortgage – smaller relative risks are still meaningful.

HOW TO FIGURE A RELATIVE RISK:	Step 1: Figure the percentage of people "at risk" by group. For instance, this could be the denial rate for blacks versus whites. Step 2: Divide the two numbers. The numerator ought to be the group you focus on in your reporting. In this case, it's black applicants. Step 3: Decide how to express it. Your choices are as a ratio ("as likely") or as a percent difference ("more likely"). Make any calculations you need to match your words and numbers.
FORMULA:	Step 1: (number affected / total in group 1), (number affected / total in group 2) Step 2: Divide the two (Answer group 1 / Answer Group 2) Step 3: Convert to a percentage if it's less than 2, express as a ratio if it's more than 2. If you convert it to a percentage difference, express as "percent more (or less) likely than": (relative risk-1) x 100.

EXAMPLE: In Nashville, 40 of 120 upper-income black home loan applicants were denied mortgages; 300 of 2,400 whites in the same income bracket were denied loans.

Step 1: Figure the denial rates:

Blacks = 40 / 120 = .33333, or 33.3 percent, or one-third.

Whites = 300 / 2,400 = .125 or 12.5 percent, or one-eighth.

Step 2: Figure out the relative risk:

.333 / .125 = 2.664

In words, this says, "Upper income blacks are denied for mortgages 2 1/2 times the rate of whites."

Step 3: Change how it's expressed to allow for the words "more likely" by calculating a percent change without multiplying by 100. (See "Measuring change" for more on percent changes.):

(33.3-12.5) / 12.5 = 1.664

In words this says, "Blacks are 1.7 times more likely than whites to be denied for loans."

A NOTE ON SIGNIFICANCE TESTING AND RATES

Reporters often ask how they can tell a significant difference in rates from a meaningless one. For example, if police use force on black youths 6 percent of the time they arrest them, but on whites only 5 percent of the time, is that a significant difference?

It probably doesn't matter.

First, journalists rarely work with samples. Statistical significance is most important in polls and other surveys, which randomly select some people to represent others.

Most reporters would look at every use of force form, not every 10th form. That means anything you find actually happened. There's no point in comparing it to what you'd know if you had the whole universe. Just stick to what you know. In this example, you might say that police used force on black youths 20 percent more often in a single year in a single city – don't generalize to other years and other cities.

But the statistical tests are still useful to see whether your answers might be flukes of time or place. They also alert you that you may be focusing on something that seems like a big difference, but is actually quite possible because of dumb luck.

"Significant," however, doesn't mean "meaningful" or "newsworthy." All it means is, "How often would a difference like this happen by chance alone?" And given the numbers reporters deal with, it will usually come out statistically significant, even if it's meaningless. There's a strong argument that our hypothetical use of force example – a rare event that results in relatively small relative risks – is meaningless, even though it would be statistically significant and true.

The reason is that the main number that tells you whether differences in rates would happen by chance, called a chi-square, is sensitive to two things: The difference between the rates and the number of people they represent. In news, almost everything is measured off of a large base. So even minor, trivial differences between the rates often appear "significant."

This booklet won't go through calculating a chi-square. But consider turning to Philip Meyer's "New Precision Journalism" for instructions on it. For rare events like fatal accidents, police shootings or cancers, look up a primer on Poisson distributions instead of chi-square. A Poisson distribution tells you the probability that you would get a certain frequency of a rare event by chance alone. (One of its first uses was by a Prussian general who wanted to know whether deaths by horse kicks in one unit were flukes or whether something was actually wrong.) It is used when the sample size is large, but the number of positives is small and discrete.

MEASURING CHANGE

We often write about change or difference, usually as a difference between place or time.

SIMPLE DIFFERENCES (OR ACTUAL CHANGE)

A simple difference is just the result of subtracting one number from another. If you are measuring differences in time, it's the newer number minus the older number.

One time to think about using simple changes is when an event is rare, but there's a consensus that it shouldn't happen. Recent examples include the 32 crashes attributed to GM's faulty ignition switch, or the 64 deaths that the Centers for Disease Control associated with pharmacy compounding errors in 2012.

Another time to use a raw number is when it is quite understandable without any calculations. Prices of common household goods, salaries and home prices are examples of numbers that needn't always be put into perspective using percentage changes.

Finally, we work in news. That means that sometimes you'll use a raw number when it's more newsworthy. This doesn't necessarily mean the number is more alarming – just more meaningful.

INSTRUCTIONS FOR A DIFFERENCE:	Subtract the older number from the newer number. This is not the same as subtracting the little number from the big number. If a number has fallen you get a negative number. If a number has risen you get a positive number.
FORMULA:	New – Old.
EXAMPLE:	An executive made $2.4 million last year. He made $2.9 million this year. His raise was: $2.9 – $2.4 = 0.5 million, or $500,000, or half a million dollars.

PERCENT CHANGE, OR PERCENT DIFFERENCE

The most butchered form of newsroom math is the percent difference, or the percent change.

Part of the problem is that there seem to be five or six different ways to do percentage changes. Unfortunately, only two of them work every time. I'll give you the one that is easiest to understand and remember.

Note that the way we're doing this, it doesn't matter which number is bigger. If the number has *fallen*, you'll get a *negative* percent change. If the number has *risen*, you'll get a *positive* percent change. And it still comes out right if the change is bigger than 100 percent.

INSTRUCTIONS FOR A PERCENT DIFFERENCE:	Step 1: Subtract the older number from the newer number. It doesn't matter which one is bigger!
	Step 2: Divide the answer by the older number.
	Step 3: Multiply by 100, or move the decimal point two places to the right.
	Step 4: Round off and simplify.

FORMULA:	Step 1: New – Old = Difference
	Step 2: Difference / Old = Decimal answer
	Step 3: Decimal x 100 = percentage difference
	Step 4: Round off.
EXAMPLE:	An executive made $2.4 million last year. He made $2.9 million in this year.
	Step 1: Difference = $2.9 – $2.4 = $0.5 million.
	Step 2: Difference / Original number = 0.5 / $2.4 = .208
	Step 3: Move the decimal point = 20.8%
	Step 4: Round off and simplify: 21% = 21 / 100 = about 20 / 100 = 1 / 5,
	So, the executive got a raise equivalent to one-fifth of his original salary.

ACTUAL CHANGE VS. PERCENTAGE CHANGE

There's considerable disagreement in newsrooms over which measure of change is more appropriate: actual change or percentage change. The reason is that it's a news decision, not a rule.

Consider this iron-clad rule from "Statistical Deception at Work":

To be compared, percentages must grow from a similar sized base.

Most reporters who have dealt with budgets, economic growth or similar beats that stress change – or the lack of it – would reverse this rule. They would say, "When numbers are of a different scale, the only way to compare them is with percentages."

So which should you use? The actual change or the percent change? The answer: Whichever one is more newsworthy. This doesn't mean it's the biggest. A newsworthy number can be meaningful and not alarming. Of course, you should be clear which you're using: Absolute numbers, percentage change or something else.

Take a typical story produced in newsrooms around the nation: The salaries and perks for chief executives.

In Florida, where I was doing this story in the 1990s, many CEOs own most of their companies and restrict their pay. It's common to see an executive earn a modest $50,000 one year, only to increase his salary to a more respectable $100,000 when the business gets off the ground. It was also common to see executives in large utilities and elsewhere take in $2 million, with bonuses producing raises of $200,000 almost every year.

Which is more newsworthy? The 100 percent increase or the $200,000 raise? In writing these stories, I've said, "It depends." It depends on what the executives are doing, whether the companies are doing well and whether they're the biggest raises in the group.

In fact, a $2 million pay package in Florida was often more newsworthy than either of the raises.

REVERSING PERCENT DIFFERENCES

Remember that a number can grow many times, but it can only fall 100 percent to zero. This is a rough concept until you think it through. If you double a price of $20, increasing it by 100%, it's $40. If you triple it, it's $60. But if you reduce the $40 back to $20, it's a 50 percent drop, to one-half the level, not a 100 percent decrease. In other words, percent changes can't be reversed.

This means that the ads claiming you'll use three times less detergent or a food contains three times less salt are wrong and impossible. What they probably mean is that it would be three times as much if you used the other brand or ate the other food, or the brand is one third as much. Here are two ways this makes a difference:

MATCHING PERCENTAGE CHANGES:	If the budget for police grows by 15 percent one year, then falls by 15 percent, it doesn't get back to where it started – it falls to a lower level.
HERE'S HOW IT WORKS:	Step 1: $1 million grows by 15 percent: $1 million + (15% of $1 million) = $1 million + ($1,000,000 x .15) = $1 million + $150,000 = $1,150,000. Step 2: $1,150,000 falls by 15 percent, or $1,150,000 – (15% of $1,150,000) = $1,150,000 – $172,500 = $977,500. The reason this happens is that the percent is coming off of a bigger base than it grew from.

RETURNING TO THE SAME LEVEL YOU STARTED FROM:	A number that goes back to the same level it started from also doesn't have matching percentage changes. A number bigger than zero can't fall more than 100 percent, but it can rise as many percents as you need.
	Step 1: $1 million triples to $3 million. The percent change is ($3-1) / 1 = 2, or a 200 percent increase. (We often express this as "triple the level" instead of calculating the percent change.)
	Step 2: $3 million falls to $1 million. The percent change is ($1 − 3) / 3 = -.667, a 67 percent drop, or the value fell by two-thirds.

(It's actually impossible to calculate the percent change of a number that changes signs. This comes up in earnings reports, in which a company lost money one year and made money the next. That's not a valid calculation.

For example, if earnings went from -$200 to $100, you'd get a 300 percent increase. But you'd also get a 300 percent increase if it went from 25 to 100, which is the only time that the answer is right. Going the other way, you'd get a -300 percent change, which is also impossible and wrong.

PERCENTAGE POINT DIFFERENCE VS. PERCENT DIFFERENCE – ONE WORD: BIG DIFFERENCE

Describing changes in percentages creates confusion and disagreement in newsrooms. Here are two examples, both correct:

• Population growth has slowed by about 1.3 percentage points since its peak in 1950, to 0.7 percent. (Simple difference between 2 percent and 0.7 percent, expressed in percentage points.)

• Population growth in the U.S. slowed by almost two-thirds from its peak in 1950, to 0.7 percent in 2013. (Percent difference between 2 percent and 0.7 percent)

A.K. Dewdney, author of "200 Percent of Nothing," calls the latter method, "percentage pumping." He says it's an illegitimate way to make a minor change look significant.

Others disagree, particularly those who study investments and medicine. We've been taught for years that it's not fair to calculate a percent difference between two percentages. If you look back at the last section, though, that's exactly what a relative risk does. Logarithms in algebra and derivatives in calculus are other ways to express the same idea.

There are two times when calculating a percent difference of a percentage or rate can help clarify, rather than mystify, a number.

First, it helps when the values begin at very different levels. For example, the violent crime rate in Maryland was nearly three times the rate in Virginia in the 1980s. Comparing trends, it would be impossible for Virginia to improve as much as Maryland in percentage point terms. Its crime rate fell more than the total crime in Virginia.

Second, it helps when you're dealing with rare events, as in the relative risk we discussed earlier.

The right answer is up to you. You can stress change or the lack of it. But make your decision based on the meaning in your story, not on the more alarming of the two figures. And be sure to use the proper language to describe what you've done.

GOING FURTHER WITH CHANGES: ANNUAL RATES AND INFLATION ADJUSTMENT

ANNUAL RATES

We rarely calculate annual rates in the newsroom, but it's a useful calculation, especially if you want to deconstruct the numbers that others give you.

Back in 1996, vice presidential candidate Jack Kemp argued that his proposed flat tax and a series of other tax cuts would spur the economy to grow at a 5 percent annual rate. He compared it with the 60 percent in the nation's economy from the late 1950s to the late 1960s. The implication was that this goal was achievable.

Kemp may have depended on a reasonable person's attempt to figure out what 60 percent over a decade meant. And the logical conclusion among most Americans, including journalists, was that it grew 6 percent a year.

Not so. Whenever you look at changes over a long time, it's important to figure out annual rates. The compounding effect is the same principle that lets your nest egg grow a lot even if you start with a small account in a mutual fund.

There are two times you'll need to know how to figure out annualized changes.

First, you'll need it to project recent changes in the future. Second, you'll need it to figure out how a change over a long time translates into an average each year. They're based on the same principle, and you'll have to deal with exponents. If this repels you, feel free to skip over this section for now. You can come back to it when the need arises.

PROJECTING ANNUAL RATES FORWARD

PROJECTING CURRENT CHANGES TO THE FUTURE:	You can always make little changes look big by projecting numbers forward over a lot of years. So can your sources. Here's how they do it: Step 1: Divide the current number by last year's number. What you get is an answer above 1 if the current number has grown, below 1 if it shrank. This answer is the ratio of this year's number to last year's number. We'll call it a ratio. Step 2: Raise the ratio to the power that equals the number of years you care about. This is the same as multiplying your answer by itself 10 times for 10 years. Step 3: Multiply this answer by the original value to find the future value, then make any calculations you need from there.
FORMULA:	Step 1: (New/Old) = Ratio Step 2: Ratio# years = Multiplier Step 3: Multiplier x old value = Future value Step 4: Use this answer to calculate anything else you need, such as the percent change from now until some time in the future.

EXAMPLE:	The budget of a small town, rose from $144.3 million to $149.6 million last year. How much would it rise over a decade if it kept up this rate?
	Step 1: (New / Old) = 149.6 / 144.3 = 1.03672..... This is equivalent to a 3.7 percent increase.
	Step 2: Answer to the 10th power: = (1.03672)10 = 1.43434...
	To raise a number to a power on a calculator, look for a button that looks something like yx. Enter the number that you want raised (1.03672 in this example), press that button, and then enter the number of years (10).
	To raise a number to a power on a spreadsheet, use the caret symbol (^): =1.03672^10. Computer languages often use two asterisks (**) to indicate a power calculation. This is one of the basic "operators" used in every programming language, so look for that term in the documentation if these don't work.
	Step 3: Multiply the answer by last year's value: 1.43434... x 144.3 = $207 million
	Step 4: Make other calculations, such as the total percent change: ($207-144.3) / 144.3 = 0.43, or a 43 percent increase.

CONVERTING TOTAL CHANGE TO ANNUAL RATES

Neill Borowski, former director of computer-assisted reporting and
analysis at The Philadelphia Inquirer, used annual rates in a local story
on the cost of homes, even when he couldn't get reliable value estimates
for every house through property tax records. Instead, he figured out
how much each house had increased in price when it was sold, and then
figured out an average annual rate from there.

Working backward would also help you with the Jack Kemp example.
In fact, you might make a habit of converting any totals that refer to
more than a few years into annual rates. It often makes them look less
impressive.

FIGURING ANNUAL RATES:	Step 1: Divide the new number by the old number or convert a known percentage change to a ratio by moving the decimal place back over to the left (dividing by 100) and adding 1.
	Step 2: Raise that to 1 / the number of years. There's no simple manual equivalent of doing this, since you're taking the nth root of the number. (In other words, what times itself for 10 times will give you the number you need?)
	Step 3: Convert it back to a percentage by subtracting 1 and moving the decimal place over to the right.

FORMULA:	Step 1: Total Ratio = (New / Old) or Total Ratio = (Total percent change / 100) + 1. Step 2: Annual ratio = Total Ratio (1 / # years) Step 3: Annual percent change = (1 – Annual Ratio) x 100
EXAMPLE:	Using our example from Jack Kemp, you can do either of these two: Step 1: GDP 1968 / GDP 1958 = ($3293.9 / 2057.5) = 1.601 or ((Percent change 1958 to 1968 / 100) + 1) = (60.1 /100) + 1 = 1.601 Step 2: Raise to the 1/10th power = 1.601 (1/10) = 1.048 Step 3: Subtract 1 and move the decimal place = (1.048 – 1) = 0.048, or 4.8 percent annual rate. So during the fastest period of economic growth in modern history, the U.S. economy didn't match Kemp's goal. And this doesn't take into account rapid population growth, post-War buildups or other factors that are not expected to reoccur.

ADJUSTING FOR INFLATION

When you compare two things measured in dollars over a long time, you should usually adjust your figures for inflation.

Most reporters and experts alike agree that it's unfair to compare salaries in the 2000s with those in the 1970s if you don't take inflation into account. Other subjects get murkier. In government finance, budget cuts might be after inflation (which would indicate a small increase in the actual value), or before inflation (which would be an absolute dollar cut). A source's political leanings may determine which choice is made, and you should be sure to ask.

Reporters should use whichever value makes sense in the story. But if you're comparing numbers over more than about five years, it's customary to adjust them for inflation or anticipated inflation. Be sure to adjust anything you think might be record-breaking, such as an all-time high gasoline price.

Don't let reports of problems in the Consumer Price Index stop you from performing this simple check on the value of money. It's better than nothing. And most alternatives are derived from the CPI and could have the same problems.

If you wanted to get picky, you might look at inflation indexes produced by the Bureau of Economic Analysis, an arm of the Commerce Department. They're called Implicit Price Deflators, and are calculated using a combination of detailed CPI results and the figures that are used to compute the Gross Domestic Product. The closest match to the CPI is a deflator for "consumer expenditures." Another one computes price changes in government expenditures, and is useful for working with city budgets.

These are often considered the most conservative estimates of inflation because they reverse some of the problems with the CPI. But don't get too tied up in details. All government inflation estimates show the same long-term trends.

Most news organizations express results in the current year. Economists more frequently use the "base year" of the index. The justification for rejecting academic standards is that our readers have a hard time picturing value 5 or 10 years ago, but know what a dollar is worth today.

You'll often see these calculations referred to as "real dollars" or "constant dollars." For example, the Bureau of Economic Analysis reports the "real Gross Domestic Product." When you see the word "real" or "constant" before the word "dollars," you are looking at numbers that have already been adjusted for inflation.

In reports, statisticians may say that a figure is expressed in "billions of chained 2009 dollars" or something like it. These are also already adjusted for inflation, but they are expressed in the value of money in 2009 rather than today.

If you see the phrase, "current dollars," the answer isn't already and you ought to do it yourself.

HOW TO ADJUST FOR INFLATION:	You need three pieces of information to adjust for inflation: the ratio of prices in one period (now) to the prices in another period (then) and the value in the past (then).
	Most people use the Consumer Price Index for All Urban Consumers from the Bureau of Labor Statistics, which it calls the CPI-U (all items, not seasonally adjusted), with the most recent base period available. For one figure, BLS has an inflation calculator on its website. To get the historical data so you can apply the formula to lots of numbers, look under its "top picks" under Data Tools or within Prices and Inflation.
	Step 1: Divide the latest year's CPI by the CPI for the year of your earlier data.
	Step 2: Multiply the answer by the dollar figure for the year you want to adjust.
FORMULA:	Step 1: Ratio of prices now to prices then = (CPI Now / CPI Then)
	Step 2: Multiply by old value: Answer x Value then
	A more complex version would use another period as a base: That is,
	Adjusted value = (CPI Year / CPI Base) x Values in the corresponding years. You'd have to do this with both the previous and the current numbers to get the comparable values.

EXAMPLE: Teachers made about $9,000 in 1970. In 2012 they made $54,000. Is that a big raise or a little one?

Step 1: Get the ratio of prices in 2012 to prices in 1970 using the CPI-U for All Items (All cities). This is 229.6 / 38.8 = 5.9175. This means it took about $6 in 2012 to buy what people bought for $1 in 1970.

Step 2: Apply the answer to the original salary by multiplying: 5.9175 x $9,000 = $53,257.

This means that, after inflation, the average teacher got a raise of $54,000 – $53,257, or about $750. So there's not much difference in salaries over 26 years, once inflation is factored out.

Notice that this is expressed in numbers your readers will understand – everything is in the latest year's dollars.

UNDERSTANDING AVERAGES – MEANS, MEDIANS AND MODES

Averages are just summaries. If a quote sums up an event, or an anecdote sums up a person using his actions instead of words, an average sums up a human condition of some kind – money, congestion, death or disease – in a single number.

Choosing your average carefully or deciding there may be another number or method to sum up a situation can mean the difference between accurately and inaccurately describing your story.

In fact, understanding different kinds of averages – what they tell us and what they don't – is the first thing you learn in basic statistics classes. If an average doesn't summarize your data well, it's not very productive to move forward into many other kinds of analysis. There are three basic types of averages.

A mean is the simple average – one computed by adding values and dividing that sum by the number of items you added together. A median is the middle value, often called "typical" in news. A mode is the most common value.

THE SIMPLE AVERAGE, OR MEAN

A simple average, also called the arithmetic mean, is the kind that you see most frequently in the news. It's most descriptive when it averages numbers that don't vary too much at either the top or bottom ends. These averages will often be misleading when they refer to items measured in dollar amount like incomes, housing costs and the like.

CALCULATING A SIMPLE AVERAGE OR MEAN:	Step 1: Add up a list of numbers. Step 2: Divide the answer by the number of numbers you've added up.
FORMULA FOR SIMPLE AVERAGES:	Step 1: Sum of numbers Step 2: Sum / Count of numbers For spreadsheet users: =AVERAGE(list of numbers)

EXAMPLE:	Here are five home prices on a block:
	
	    $75,000 $100,000
	    $75,000 $350,000
	    $95,000
	
	Step 1: 75,000 +75,000 +95,000 +100,000 +350,000 = 695,000
	
	Step 2: 695,000 / 5 = 139,000. So the average home price is more than all but one on the list.

MEDIANS OR MIDDLE VALUES

Medians are often used to summarize the value of things measured in dollars, especially home prices and incomes. The reason is that they are not sensitive to one or two unusually high or low values the way the average in the previous example is.

But it's harder to get a median because you need a list of all values. For example, if you know the total income of a metropolitan area and the number of people in that area, you can compute the average – or per capita income – but not the median.

If you need a median, then, you either need to learn a little computer-assisted reporting or get a friendly source to give it to you. One way to express the median is to call it the "typical" value. Another way is to say that it's the "middle" value.

CALCULATING A MEDIAN:	To get the median, list all of your numbers in order, beginning with the lowest and ending with the highest.
	Count how many numbers you have and divide by two.
	Now add 0.5. If that comes out to a whole number (like 13), count up the list that many values. If it's not (like 12.5), take the average of the two numbers surrounding the number. (For 24 items in a list, the number would be 24/2 + .5, or 12.5. So take the average of the 12th and 13th item on your list.).
	In other words, this is the closest you can get to the middle of the list. This is a sorting and counting job, not a calculator job.
	In a spreadsheet, use the =MEDIAN() function. Most programming languages also have a median function, but you may have to install a math package for languages like Python or Ruby. Relational databases like Microsoft Access or MySQL don't have a median function and different flavors of SQL will require different workarounds.

EXAMPLE:	Here are the same five home prices on a block: $75,000 $75,000 $95,000 $100,000 $350,000 The median is $95,000, or the 3rd value on the list (5 prices / 2 = 2.5, + 0.5 = 3, so take the third value. Compare this to the average we calculated in the last section of $141,000. Which one more accurately describes the list in a single number?

MODES OR COMMON VALUES

The mode is the most common value. It's rarely used in news except during elections and in polling. Use it to find a single item that's the most popular, not to summarize a large list of numbers.

For example, the winner of an election is the "modal" candidate: she got "the most" votes. This isn't the same as the majority of votes – it could be under 50 percent, even if it's the most.

The mode of our list of house values is $75,000.

IS ANYONE AVERAGE?

When readers or viewers hear the word, "average," they tend to figure that you're talking about the typical person.

But with home prices, salaries and other dollar figures, you'll usually be painting a picture of someone with means well beyond the typical person.

In other words, you'll usually paint a particularly inaccurate picture, or unfairly summarize, the data.

As a rule of thumb, use the average when it's similar to the median. Use the median when they're very different. When you have a lot of actual values, the mode isn't very useful. But if you can put the values into ranges, like "Under $100,000," then it can be telling.

Here's an example, using baseball player salaries for 2013, grouped into ranges of values:

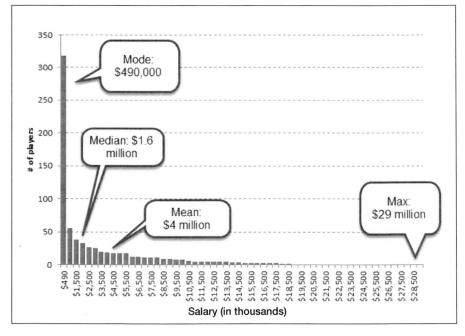

(The averages shown are from the actual list, not the groups.)

The simple average might be the appropriate summary if the story dealt with the cost of players to owners. But if the story described the conditions (or wealth) of the players, the median might be best. To talk about the most common experiences, the mode – which here represents the minimum salary in Major League Baseball that year – could be even better.

Sometimes no single number adequately paints your picture. This often happens with something called bimodal distributions. These sets of numbers would have two clumps in the chart above, one at the top and one at the bottom with a dip in the middle.

It's often difficult to summarize numbers that measure people, children, building trends or anything else affected by the Baby Boom.

For example, elementary school enrollments swelled to 34 million students in 1968, fell back to 27 million in 1986, and swelled again to 31 million in the late 1990s. The average of 29.9 million doesn't accurately reflect any period, even though it's close to the median of 30.2. You may need two numbers instead of one.

One technique for dealing with distributions that don't lend themselves to easy averages is to use quartiles . This splits the numbers into four groups, each with an equal number of members. It's the same idea as a median, but gives you a little more description.

GOING FURTHER WITH CENTRAL TENDENCY: AVERAGING AVERAGES, CHANGES AND SIGNIFICANCE

THE PROBLEM OF AVERAGING AVERAGES

WEIGHTED AVERAGES

You usually can't take a bunch of averages and make an average of them to get anything of meaning. Here's an example:

	EMPLOYEES	AVERAGE SALARY
TEACHER	10,000	$37,000
CUSTODIAN	2,000	$20,000
PRINCIPAL	500	$75,000
SIMPLE AVERAGE		$44,000

This average doesn't take into account that the number of employees under different job titles is very different.

The true average salary would repeat the $37,000 10,000 times, then repeat the $75,000 500 times, then repeat the $20,000 2,000 times. Adding all of those up, and dividing by the number of employees, would give you the true average.

To do that, you'll use multiplication:

	EMPLOYEES		SALARY	
TEACHER	10,000	X	$37,000	= $370,000,000
CUSTODIAN	2,000	X	$20,000	= $40,000,000
PRINCIPAL	500	X	$75,000	= $37,500,000
SUM	12,500			= $447,500,000
WEIGHTED AVERAGE			$35,800	

Dividing 447,500,000 / 12,500 (the sum of the money divided by the number of people) gives you an average salary of $35,800 – about what you'd expect. This isn't just an estimate of the average; mathematically, it works out that it's the same number you'd get if you had the full list.

GROUPED MEDIANS

You can't find the median group from a list of numbers like the one we had above. To even get an approximate number, you'd need a different list: The number of employees by salary range, regardless of their titles.

You'd list them in ascending order and create a column with a running total for the number of employees. At the end, you'll have the total number of employees which you divide by two, add 0.5 and then find the group that includes that number in the running total column:

SALARY RANGE	EMPLOYEES	RUNNING TOTAL
0-$20,000	2,000	2,000
$21,000-$30,000	6,000	8,000
$31,000-$40,000	4,000	12,000
$41,000-$50,000	250	12,250
$51,000 AND UP	250	12,500
TOTAL	12,500	

This group spans the average of the 6,250th and 6,251st person

WORKING WITH AVERAGES AND RATES

Averaging averages sometimes gives you new insights when working with rates. For example, if you have a list of crime rates in different cities, it may be preferable to quote the "average crime rate" for all cities rather than what is essentially the total crime rate in the country. Just remember that they're different, and watch your language carefully here. Here's an example, using crime rates for 20 large cities in 2012, according to the FBI's Uniform Crime Report:

City	Population	Crimes	Rate per thousand
New York	8,289,415	195,753	24
Los Angeles	3,855,122	106,025	28
Houston	2,177,273	129,288	59
Philadelphia	1,538,957	74,850	49
Phoenix	1,485,509	70,235	47
Las Vegas	1,479,393	58,025	39
San Antonio	1,380,123	89,611	65
San Diego	1,338,477	37,229	28
Dallas	1,241,549	62,680	50
San Jose	976,459	32,010	33
Jacksonville	840,660	39,863	47
Indianapolis	838,650	56,840	68
Austin	832,901	46,877	56
San Francisco	820,363	44,675	54
Charlotte-Mecklenburg	808,504	37,825	47
Fort Worth	770,101	37,038	48
Detroit	707,096	55,967	79
El Paso	675,536	19,270	29
Louisville Metro	666,200	32,595	49
Memphis	657,436	53,010	81
Washington	632,323	36,712	58
Total, weighted average	32,012,047	1,316,378	41
Unweighted average			49
Median			49

Note that the weighted average is a little lower than the unweighted, suggesting that bigger cities have lower crime rates. (Chicago, the third-largest city, doesn't report to the FBI crime program, but it has higher crime rates – a fact that you'd need to address if you were to write about these comparisons.)

Which to use depends on the story.

If you want to compare your city to other cities, you may prefer to use the average of the rates. Otherwise, the average is artificially lowered by the low rates of the largest cities. But if you want to compare your people in your city to people who live in other big cities, then it's important to include the measure of size implied with the true average, or the total line.

This depends on what researchers call the "unit of analysis". If your focus is on big-city police departments, then you would probably prefer to compare the performance of cities. If your focus is on city residents feeling victimized, you might prefer to use the total of the group.

Researchers usually use median rather than average when they work with averages of rates.

Make especially sure you understand which you've gotten when you're working with figures from sources. They can be considerably different:

- A total, or average for the group, is often largely influenced by one or two very large components, such as Los Angeles and New York in the figures above. In a weighted average, these two cities make up more than one-third of the total. If they have unusual figures, you may end up just comparing your city or your number to these large groups.

- An average of an average has the opposite problem. It counts a small area or small group as just as important as a big one. It also can be influenced by one "outlier" from a small group – perhaps the high crime rate in Memphis in the example above.

- A median of the rates can still be influenced by a small group, but much less so. That's why researchers often use it.

SOME FIGURES TO TROUBLESHOOT YOUR AVERAGES

Statisticians use some standard tools to troubleshoot averages. That's because averages are so important to every test they run that they need to become fully aware of any problems. Their goal, though, is the same as a journalist's: Does a simple average accurately summarize many of the values you see in the real world? If not, then further analysis may be worthless.

Arming yourself with statisticians' tools is one way to troubleshoot averages.

STANDARD DEVIATION

A standard deviation tells you how closely all the values are clustered around an average.

A very large standard deviation (say, a value as big or bigger than the average itself for positive numbers) means that hardly anyone is average. There is probably a clump of people, for example, earning $50,000 and one earning $150,000. In our baseball salary example above, recall that the average salary was $3.3 million. The standard deviation is $4.5 million – considerably more than the average. And the average was, indeed, misleading.

A more moderate standard deviation (say, a value somewhat smaller than average itself for a list of numbers that don't fall below zero) means that it's pretty typical and expected – the list of values falls around something closer to the ordinary bell curve that represents a normal binomial distribution. In this case, the average follows the expected rules of statistics. Physical characteristics like height and weight follow this pattern. So do test scores like SAT's and IQ – those tests are created to always follow it. In a perfect normal distribution, the median is the same as the mean.

A very small standard deviation (a value very close to zero) means there's not much difference among the numbers you're examining. This could mean they're not very interesting. For example, if the average test score is 98 in school reports, and the standard deviation is 1, then virtually all test scores are between 96 and 100. The test may not be measuring any meaningful difference among students.

TRIMMED MEAN

This value is "trimmed" of the extreme numbers. It usually takes the middle 95 percent of the figures, ignoring the very, very high and the very, very low numbers. It often comes out to something much closer to the median. You can choose how much to trim. Some people only trim the top and bottom 1 or 2 percent.

HISTOGRAMS

The chart we saw on the baseball salaries is called a histogram, which will help you picture how your values are spread out. This kind of chart counts up how many of your values fall within ranges that you define. (You can also let the software decide for you in R and some other packages.) Here's an example of a skewed distribution, in which all of the values are smushed into one corner.

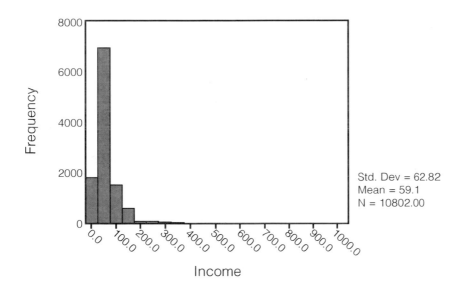

Std. Dev = 62.82
Mean = 59.1
N = 10802.00

This is a graph of incomes in the Nashville, Tenn., area. The "frequency" is the number of people in each income group. You can hardly see it, but some home mortgage applicants have incomes as high as $1 million.

But most of the values – about 7,000 of them – are around $40,000 (the value that would be between 0 and 100 in the horizontal part of the chart).

You can also see that our statistical software gives us a way to see it in numbers: It lists the mean (or average) and the standard deviation. The standard deviation is higher than the average. Another standard plot to troubleshoot averages – usually when you compare groups like men vs. women – is called a boxplot. It contains a lot of information in a little chart and is worth looking up if you find yourself working with grouped averages.

This is a rather simplistic way of viewing what statisticians call "univariate analysis". Consider getting an elementary statistics book or taking an introductory online statistics course to learn more.

THE PROBLEM OF COMPARING AVERAGES OVER TIME

Be careful when comparing averages over time. In many cases, these averages reflect different items creating apples-to-oranges comparisons. Let's take the median home price as an example.

Each month, various government agencies and trade associations release analyses of home prices. Sometimes they're prices of new homes, sometimes they're prices of existing homes sold that month. They're never the value of all homes, since no one knows that for the nation.

The problems in these numbers include what is called weighting and quality adjustment

Each house sold or built counts for one element in the number, whether it's a median or a simple average. But the mix of homes sold changes each month. So it's possible these surveys are just measuring the change in the size of homes (quality adjustment), or the popularity of city versus suburbs, or California versus Iowa (weighting), rather than the value of typical home.

Other stories that suffer from similar problems include death rates at hospitals, executive pay in companies and school reports.

For example, comparing death rates across states could end up just comparing the age of people in each state, not the health of its residents.

Some professional specialties have standard adjustments they make to these measures to account for changes. Death rates, for instance, are almost always reported on an age-adjusted basis. Sometimes researchers narrow their investigations to a single age group to accommodate this problem – people in their 50s are a popular target for such narrowing. Other times, they choose a typical mix of old and young and apply the death rates to those groups. Then they add up the deaths for this standard population.

But home prices are rarely compared so scientifically.

That means we're stuck: Either report on a flawed number or report no number on an issue that represents the biggest single asset or investment the typical family will ever have.

Reporting nothing simply isn't an option for most of us. So how can you characterize the number when it has such a great potential for error?

One alternative is to report it as "the best available measure of the value of homes," and include a short paragraph at the end of the story warning that the mix of homes changes each month, so the numbers can change even if no value has changed.

CHAPTER 3:
Working with Graphics

We're used to the idea that visualizing data is often times more effective than writing with numbers. The tools available to even the least technical among us have made it possible to, in a few minutes; transform your data into visuals.

Stephen Few, a consultant on visual display of business-related data, describes several types of uses in which a good graphic will let a reader understand data better than in words or numbers. These include getting good overview or birds' eye view of the data; rapidly comparing values; and seeing or comparing trends and patterns.

Media critics complain that news graphics are misleading, though their voices are becoming more muted. That comes, in part, from the vast resources available to journalists who want to tackle visualization, including sophisticated tools that suggest good design practices and accessible examples like Nathan Yau's Flowing Data website. Edward Tufte, a Yale professor, publishes his own coffee-table books on informational graphics. Get them.

But these and other resources don't always address the problems faced in reporting. Here, I'll review a few of the most basic guidelines for creating static visualizations that might help you see patterns you'd otherwise miss. I'll avoid mentioning particular tools or programming languages as much as possible because they change so frequently (remember Flash?). Many of these techniques are possible in a spreadsheet, but the versatility of the R programming language and other tools could tempt you to become more proficient.

TYPES OF CHARTS

Books and examples (more here and here) will help you decide
what kind of chart to make with what kind of data. Visualize This!,
by Nathan Yau, is a good primer. Here, are a few other things to
consider when you're creating your exploratory visualizations.

AVOIDING MISIMPRESSIONS

One kind of graphic that's easy to misinterpret shows percent
changes on a fever or line chart.

Look at the difference in how you'd interpret these two graphics,
which both show the change in the population of the New York
metropolitan area over six years.

This first graphic – a bar chart – makes it clear that the population
continued to rise in the 1990s, but at a slower rate than in the
early 1990s.

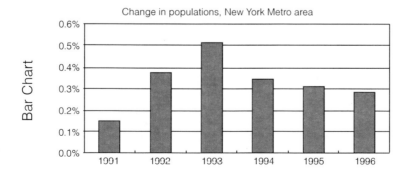

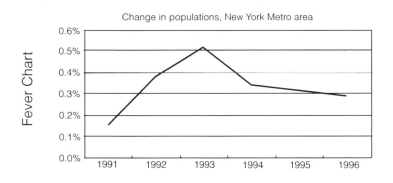

The immediate reaction to this fever chart, despite clear labeling, is that the population has fallen because the line is going down. There's no visual clue, the way there is with a bar chart that is still above zero. By hinging all changes on the axis, bar charts show changes better than line charts.

Similar issues arise with graphs with categories. Unless there's a natural order to a list of items, such as time or importance, it's usually a good idea to make them horizontal rather than the vertical ones above.

Think through any graphic you produce, either on your own or with your graphics department. Make sure your first reaction matches the story as you understand it. Run it by a couple of colleagues, without any text on it, to see if they can understand it. And remember, if a first glance makes you hesitate, then think what will happen to your colleagues, readers or viewers.

SMALL MULTIPLES AND SPARKLINES

Tufte has advocated two techniques that are worth trying early in a story. The first is to create what he calls small multiples – the same chart produced very small over and over using different groups. They might be counties, types of grant programs or classifications of workers. Putting them all together makes it easy to see differences because once you get used to reading one, you can read them all in a glance. These are easy to produce in R and in programming languages, but difficult in Excel and other software.

This example was produced while reporting a story on the nationalization of state legislative campaigns. We wanted to see if out-of-state contributions surged in the campaign that turned power over to a single party. Once you learn to read one, you've learned to read them all:

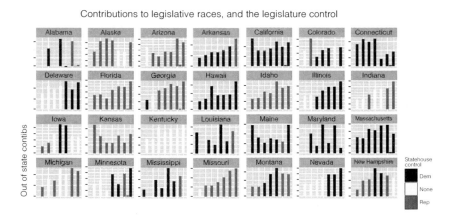

Contributions to legislative races, and the legislature control

Notice that there are no scales shown. The goal was to get a quick impression that could help lead us to interesting states, not to convey precise information. (As an aside, these numbers are not adjusted for inflation. The changes in campaign finance laws over the period shown overwhelmed any effect of the value of money.)

A related technique is built into Excel: Tufte's "sparklines," which he calls word-size graphics. He originally proposed that they replace descriptions of numeric trends within narratives, but they've instead become a standard way to compare many rows on a spreadsheet.

Here's the contribution data from the same story, with two sets of sparklines – one displayed with lines, the other with bars. Notice that you get somewhat different impressions looking at these because of the scales used.

Row Labels	2000	2002	2004	2006	2008	2010	2012	Grand Total		
CA	$2,266,183	$1,689,853	$1,111,774	$1,334,752	$1,883,304	$1,574,195	$2,026,745	$11,886,806		
TX	$1,216,272	$876,942	$893,773	$998,619	$1,439,708	$1,504,763	$1,882,099	$8,812,175		
PA	$1,070,238	$708,271	$830,084	$1,327,543	$1,535,582	$1,213,818	$1,354,282	$8,039,819		
IL	$1,320,173	$1,201,951	$650,275	$792,131	$637,331	$1,043,078	$1,393,577	$7,038,514		
NY	$481,776	$572,375	$736,652	$1,003.309	$1,115,335	$1,155,434	$1,115,500	$6,180,381		
OH	$424,996	$523,313	$311,127	$573,245	$955,527	$1,440,407	$1,450,571	$5,679,186		

MAPS

Making maps of geographic data is one of the most important skills reporters have learned in the past two decades. Nothing can replace seeing the distance between crimes, or the clustering of the wealthy in school zones.

But sometimes maps are less informative than other ways to look at geographic data. In the statehouse example above, trying to map the data would have required removing some other piece of information. And U.S. maps, in particular, can show patterns that are atypical of the country because of the large low-population areas in the mountain states and the northern plains. North Dakota, with its single congressional district, often looks like a monolith on electoral maps. During the 2012 election, NPR and The New York Times published maps, but their primary exploratory and analytic interactives did not stress geography.

That said, placing data geographically on an interactive graphic helps readers navigate to the area they care about, and they are especially useful to decide where reporters should go to find Ground Zero of their story.

THE PROBLEM OF SCALE

Graphics are designed to convey information, not hide it. Some of the rules used in newsrooms don't help achieve that goal. The one that causes the most problems is the scale of the Y-axis, or the one with numbers rather than words.

Many authors on the topic of lying with statistics point to graphics as tools with which devious journalists try to fool their readers into believing sensational versions of the facts rather than the truth. Here's a typical complaint – this one from the little book that's become a bible for many journalists, "How to Lie with Statistics":

> ... suppose you want to win an argument, shock a reader, move him into action, sell him something. For that ... chop off the bottom.

Others disagree that a reason to chop off the bottom is to alarm or deceive. Consider the Dow Jones Industrial Average, which ranged from about 13,000 to 17,000 in 2013.

Here's one way to display it:

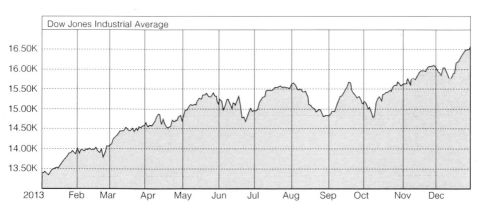

Here's a chart of weekly prices over the same period that starts at zero.

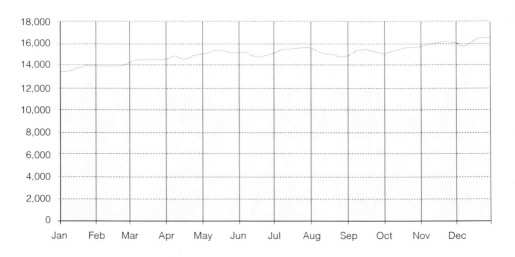

Think of the audience for this chart – attentive investors who want their information efficiently. They prefer the one that chops off the bottom.

Patrick Remington, an epidemiologist from the University of Wisconsin, also ignores the rule that a graph must begin at zero. In a presentation to journalists on understanding his craft, he showed three graphs and asked the audience to tell him which one told the story better. It's not the one that starts at zero.

Remington suggested creating a buffer of about one-third of the space of the chart at the bottom. That means if the range of values is 40-100, put one-third of the difference between the high value and the low value (or 60 /3, or 20) on either side. Make the graphic go from 40-20 (or 20) to 100+20 (or 120).

Here's how the stock market chart would look using this rule:

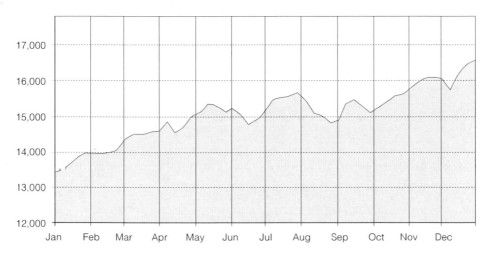

It's unreasonable to expect some values to fall to zero. In Remington's case, he knows that we will not, at least in the near future, eliminate breast cancer as a cause of death. So he also looks for a goal or a reasonable floor to the value that's based on outside research. He expands the scale to that level if the one-third rule leaves him above it.

In 1988, William Cleveland and two co-authors came up with the idea of "banking to 45," which refers to the angle at which we perceive change most clearly. It means that he was recommending that the average slope of a line in a chart be 45 degrees, or approximately the change shown in the Yahoo! chart above. Cleveland's findings on perception are built into the defaults of the R language's ggplot2 library, including recommended aspect ratios (the ratio of horizontal to vertical) and banking to 45.

When constructing your graphic, consider what experts consider important. If most experts see a 5 percent decline in the market as a meaningful and newsworthy event, then make sure your graphic relays that importance. It should mirror the real-world importance of the trend – or the lack of it.

USING VISUALIZATION AS A REPORTING TOOL

Most books and resources about data visualizations treat them as a final product for publication. The journalists already know the story they hope to tell and are looking for effective and interesting ways to present that story to readers.

But more journalists should consider using visualizations as reporting tools to help identify stories and troubleshoot data they get from sources or public records. You can do some of this in a spreadsheet, but it's easier if you learn a little of the R language, or if you sign up for one of the online services like Tableau Public.

Early in your reporting, don't obsess too much about having every number exact. You might be missing a year in a trend line, or one data point is obviously wrong. Don't worry about making it perfect – you can even hand draw a simple graphic if it's easier for you than any alternative. You'll need to fix it before publication, but you may find that you don't care enough about the picture to make it worth the effort. You'll know how hard it will be to collect the data early enough to do something about it while gaining insights for your story.

Some other tips and techniques for early reporting include:

Try looking at pictures of your data with no labels, in different sizes and with different scales. Try all different kinds of charts (as long as they're not 3-d). Each type will show you something different.

Chart your data in raw form, in percent of total or as a rate, in changes or percent changes over time, and sometimes even in logarithms and square roots of the data. You'll see something different each way. There is no rule when you're looking for patterns, and you may see something interesting that disappears when you look at it another way. You'll want to think carefully about focusing on a pattern that only appears in one or two charts.

Experiment with some of the less conventional graph types, such as a tree map, bubble charts or diff charts.

PRECISION AND ACCURACY AND INTERACTIVE VISUALIZATIONS

It's natural for us to want to publish our work and to show all of the data underneath it in an interactive graphic or news app. But before you jump into that pond, make sure that the accuracy of your data can withstand minute scrutiny. It will expose every wart in your data – problems you can write around in text or might be muted in a static graphic.

CHAPTER 4:
The Standard Stories

THE BUDGET STORY – USING PERCENTAGES, INFLATION ADJUSTMENT AND MEASURES OF CHANGE

Editors frequently want to know how to improve their coverage of local government budgets. Some reporters are trained to use spreadsheets to generate better questions for their sources during the meetings. But covering budget stories really means bringing together everything else in this book to understand the effects on readers and viewers.

Budget stories are much easier to do if you use a spreadsheet because you'll use its power to repeat calculations over and over. But it's not necessary. You can do it on a piece of paper.

UNDERSTANDING THE BUDGET

A budget is a planning document. That planning can be accurate or inaccurate. It can be responsible or irresponsible.

For example, if I planned my annual budget assuming I would get a 25 percent raise this year, you'd probably tell me I was dreaming. I ought to have a good reason to believe that before I build it in to the rent I plan to pay next year.

Along similar lines, if my family budget planned for a big drop in my costs, like a rent cut of 15 percent, you'd also say I was nuts. How could I possibly expect to convince my landlord to be so generous?

And if my insurance bill came last month announcing a 30 percent increase, I'd be irresponsible to my family if I failed to take that into account when I planned for next year.

But governments large and small take similar false premises and build them into their budgets every year in every state. So one way to look at the budget is, "Is there any reason to believe this is true accurate?"

A participant at a Florida workshop on numbers in the newsroom brought with her the budget for the school year, which had started that week. Officials were late in finalizing the document – it was going to be voted on that day. We looked through it for planning problems. There was a big one: The school district had already spent more than half of its annual budget for substitute teachers, and school had only been open for three days.

A budget is also a list of priorities that politicians fight over. They argue whether to raise taxes, reduce spending, or shift resources into fighting crime or lowering class sizes. We should treat it as such.

That means looking at how priorities have changed from recent years. It might mean covering the choices politicians have to make.

TIPS FOR PREPARING FOR THE BUDGET SEASON

Gather figures on population, inflation and past budgets to put the numbers into perspective. Use per capita (See Per Person, p. 15), inflation-adjusted (Adjusting for inflation, p. 28) numbers to show how budgets have changed over time.

Compare previous budgets to actual spending. Make lawmakers accountable for their failure to accurately plan for spending. (Measuring change, p. 22)

Be prepared to check the arithmetic in the budget. It's often times wrong.

PROPERTY TAXES AND THE DREADED "MILL" – USING RATES

Reporting on property taxes depends on the method of appraisals used in your state. At one end, New York didn't update its appraisal values in more than 50 years – property taxes depended more on when your house was built than on what it's worth. At the other end, Maryland updates its appraisals every three years on a rolling basis, with the full value of the home included in the appraisal. In the middle are states like Florida, which updates its appraisals frequently, deducts a homesteading allowance and caps increases.

FIGURING PROPERTY TAXES

There are three typical ways to change property taxes.

The most straightforward is to change the tax rate, sometimes referred to as a "millage" depending on how it's applied. These are the tax issues that get debated in county council meetings.

A second way is to adjust any market value placed on a home. This is most frequently done by homeowners who want to fight their tax bill and by local initiatives that limit the market increases reflected in the appraisals. Since everything else is an application of a formula, the only wiggle room for homeowners is to challenge any value assigned to their homes.

The third is to change the adjustments allowed on the value that's taxed rather than the home's value. A homesteading allowance reduces this amount by a fixed amount for people who live in their homes; those who live elsewhere are taxed on the full value. Some states cap the annual increase in taxable value. Others apply some sort of exemption, much like an income tax deduction, on the value. Many do both.

So the key numbers you need to figure property taxes are:

1. The value of a home, as listed in the property tax appraisal
   rolls. It doesn't matter how much it's really worth. In California,
   for example, the "market value" is the value of the home in
   1978 or when it was built or last sold. A few states skip this
   step, and go directly to No. 2.

2. The value that will be taxed, sometimes called the assessment
   or the taxable value. This is often the market value of the home
   with some adjustments.

   For example, in Florida, taxable values are reduced two ways:
   First, the value can't rise more than 3 percent a year because
   of a voter initiative that limits increases in the tax bill. Then
   the homestead exemption of $25,000 is applied to the market
   value for people who live in the homes they own. The actual
   calculation is a bit more complicated, as shown in this sample
   bill, but the idea is the same.

3. The tax rate, or a dollar value based on the assessment. If
   the home is taxed at close to its market value, this is often
   expressed as a "mil" or, alternately, a "mill", which refers to the
   tax per $1,000 of assessed value.

4. Any special rules your community has in figuring the final tax.
   Most places that make adjustments make them to the taxable
   value and not the final tax. These are called tax credits. (This is
   roughly equivalent to deductions in your personal income tax.
   You can deduct the cost of mortgage interest from your salary.
   But there are many fewer items you can take directly off your
   final tax bill.)

TWO EXAMPLES OF PROPERTY TAXES

EXAMPLE 1 MARYLAND:	In Maryland, taxes are based on the fair market value of the home, determined every three years for each home. Instead of using a millage, Maryland reduces the amount of money the house is worth and applies a percentage rate.
	Step 1: Appraisal value: An appraiser goes out and looks around, compares the house to others that have sold, and assigns a market value.
	A home was appraised at $150,000 one year and $210,000 the next.
	Step 2: If the property rose in value, divide the increase by three. Add another one of the thirds to the value each year.
	60,000 / 3 = $20,000 increase in value per year: $170,000 the first year, $190,000 the next, $210,000 for the last.
	Step 3: Reduce the appraisal to come up with assessment: Multiply the value by 0.40, or take 40 percent of the fair market value.
	For next year: $170,000 x 0.40 = $68,000
	Step 4: Apply the combined state and local tax rate, which ranges from 0.5 to 6.0 percent of the assessed value.
	For next year, $68,000 x 0.06 = $4,080

| **EXAMPLE 2 CALIFORNIA:** | Californians passed an initiative in the 1970s that froze the value of property in the tax rolls. Like in New York and a few other states, then, the only way to figure a tax on a home is to know when it was built or last sold.

This is a perfect example of a case in which a spreadsheet could help. For any change in taxes, you could figure the effects on a variety of different homeowners – those who held their homes over the entire period, those who recently built a home, and those who are thinking of buying.

Here's how you would figure the taxes of a home:

Step 1: Use last year's assessment as a base.

$40,000

Step 2: Figure out if the home was sold in the past year. If it was, then use the purchase price.

If it wasn't, then get the Consumer Price Index for California for last year and this year, and figure out the percentage increase in general prices for the state.

Sold home: $300,000;

CPI for California calculated by state officials: 160.5 last year, 157.1 the previous year.

(160.5-157.1) / 157.1 = 2.2 percent. |

| **EXAMPLE 2**
CALIFORNIA:
(CONTINUED) | Step 3: For those that were sold or built, subtract $7,000.

For those that weren't, apply either 1) the CPI change, or 2) 2 percent to the old assessment – whichever is smaller.

Sold home: $300,000 -$7,000 = $293,000.

Kept home: $40,000 x 1.02 = $40,800

Step 4: Multiply the result by the tax rate. In San Francisco, the tax rate a couple of years ago was $1.164 per $100 of value

$293,000 x 1.164 percent (or, x 0.01164) = $3,410 in taxes for the sold home.

Kept home: $40,800 x 0.01164 = $475. |

THE WEATHER STORY: EARTHQUAKES, HURRICANES AND WIND-CHILL

USING INDEXES

Reporting on weather and natural disasters is a key example of understanding, "compared to what?" in news.

If the water reaches 10 feet at one location, how far above flood stage is it? If a hurricane moves from Category One to Category Two, how much more damage is expected and what other hurricanes hit with that intensity? And if an earthquake is 5.2 on the Richter Scale, what does that mean to residents?

These are visual stories, so there's no need to put too much emphasis on the numbers. But you will need some numbers in your stories. So here's a short list of the numbers you'll typically need, what they mean and how they work. A more complete list is under "weather terms" in your style book.

EARTHQUAKES AND THE RICHTER SCALE

The Richter scale measures the intensity of an earthquake at its core. It begins at 1, but people can't really feel an earthquake smaller than a 2. The highest measure ever taken was 9.5, recorded in Chile on May 22, 1960.

But it's hard to write about a Richter reading because it's logarithmic – each step up on the Richter scale means the earthquake was 10 times worse. So a 2 is 10 times bigger than a 1, and a 3 is 10 times bigger than a 2.

It also doesn't translate well into damage, since it's measured at the point of the earthquake inside the ground, or under the ocean, not where you live.

There's another scale that you'll sometimes see that may be more useful to your readers. It's called the Mercalli scale. There are two advantages to using it. If your area has an earthquake, it tells you how much damage would occur in your area, not at the epicenter. And it is linear rather than logarithmic – a 10 is twice as bad as a five, which is also how we tend to think.

HURRICANES AND TORNADOES

Hurricane scales are much easier to understand, because they're simple numbers ranging from 1 to 5, based mostly on wind speed. Technically, this is called the Saffir-Simpson Hurricane Scale.

The smallest, a Category 1 storm, has wind speeds of 74-95 miles per hour and causes minimal damage when it hits land. An example was Danny in 1997, near the mouth of the Mississippi River.

The biggest, a Category 5 storm, has winds of more than 155 miles per hour. With a Category 5, there is little left undamaged. Small buildings and mobile homes are destroyed, trees and shrubs are blown down and most roofs cave in. A Category 5 storm that hit the U.S. was Camille, which slammed into Mississippi and Louisiana. Hurricane Katrina in 2005, which killed more than 1,800, was also a Category 5 storm, but only a Category 3 when it made landfall.

Another tornado index is called the Fujita Scale. It runs from F0 to F6, but there's never been an F6.

The reason it's used less frequently is that it's given after a tornado has passed, not while it's happening, so it's of less use in news. One of its key elements is the estimated wind speed within the tornado. And it's impossible to tell the strength of a tornado from its size. A big tornado doesn't necessarily cause a lot of damage.

HEAT INDEXES AND WIND-CHILL FACTORS

A wind-chill factor is an index, converted into a Fahrenheit scale that measures a person's heat loss based on air temperature and wind speed. The formula is pretty complex and we really don't need it.

But the key thing to remember when reporting on cold snaps is that wind-chill factors aren't the actual temperature outside – they usually show up colder than the temperature.

The same is true of heat indexes, which are derived from a series of calculations involving how an average person sweats in dry versus muggy weather. It is not made for animals, even though they are sensitive to humidity. It gives you a "feels like" temperature for different parts of the country. In some ways, it's more useful for comparing regions of the country than wind-chill factors. A heat index puts numbers into the phrase, "it's not the heat but the humidity."

STADIUMS, LAYOFFS AND THE DREADED ECONOMIC IMPACT STATEMENT

One of the thorniest problems for local government reporters is the economic impact statement. This ubiquitous document comes from lobbyists who seek tax breaks for their industries or critique new minimum wage laws and regulations as job-killers; tycoons who want a new baseball stadium; and local boosters considering tax giveaways for new businesses or touting the tourism effects of a Super Bowl. These are some of the most slippery numbers in the news, colored by the outlook of the person making the estimate or the group that paid for it.

The dirty secret is that no one knows exactly how much economic impact a policy or giveaway will create or destroy. They're models, based on what has historically happened and how various industries and regions have behaved over time.

These can be conservative or optimistic, depending on how they're calculated and whether they are using back-of-the-envelope estimates or detailed records. On one end, the Obama administration used the most conservative – and wrong – method to estimate the number of jobs "created or saved" by the $787 billion stimulus program passed in the midst of a dangerously stalled economy just after his inauguration in 2009. Instead, it should have described its counts as the number of jobs financed by the act. There is no question that some of that money created spinoff jobs. The only question is how many and where.

On the other end, some of the estimates seem made out of whole cloth. In Tampa, George Steinbrenner, then the principle owner of the New York Yankees, claimed a small stadium that was in use only six weeks a year would create more jobs than one he was simultaneously pitching to New York officials for the full season.

Another use of economic impact statements is in the other direction: the multiplying effect of losing business, such as a base closure or a plant moving offshore. This study of the effects of a Whirlpool plant closing commissioned by a union and conducted by a friendly research group called Good Jobs First, is a good example of a transparent, if self-interested, impact statement of this kind.

HOW TO DECONSTRUCT AN ECONOMIC IMPACT STATEMENT

There are usually three kinds of economic impact included in a jobs estimate. It doesn't help that different people use the same term to mean different things.

The first is the effect of the actual spending, or the amount injected into the economy: how many people will be employed by the project itself? This is the only part that was counted for the stimulus.

The second is, sometimes called the "direct" and sometimes called the "indirect" effect: how much does the project need to buy from local suppliers, who in turn will need to add jobs?

These first two elements could be considered the supply side: how much suppliers in the area will have to hire in order to do business.

The last is the most troublesome: imputed effects, sometimes called the earnings multiplier or even (again) the indirect effect. This is the demand side – the effect of having more money circulating through the local economy.

Be sure that you understand which of these effects is being used, and ask consultants or city planners to break them out for you. If they can't break them out, then you might suspect they are simply using some of the most general estimates. For instance, it's widely accepted that, nationally, every new manufacturing job will create another 6 jobs in other industries. A retail job might create half of one elsewhere. But those are national figures and are usually lower in any individual region.

You can get the source of these estimates from the Bureau of Economic Analysis. It sells metropolitan area models that break down these effects through its Regional Input-Output modeling program. It's difficult to work with, but someone in your local university should have a copy and know how to use it.

Finally, in any public works project, be careful to distinguish between the construction phase and the operation phase.

Here are some other techniques for reporting on an economic impact statement:

1. Get a sense of scale

The easiest comparison to make is to compare the economic impact claimed with the total size of your local economy. Many experts use personal income – a proxy for gross domestic product at the local level – as a measure of the dollar size of an economy. That figure also comes from the Bureau of Economic Analysis, and is available at county and metro area levels. In Rockford, Ill., a proposed sports complex was going to cost $10 million in construction costs, but the local economy was around $9 billion. That's not a very big investment for its size, so a small impact wouldn't be unreasonable. Similarly, the Tampa Bay visitor's center estimated a $3.2 billion economic impact from tourism in 2011, which comes out to about 5 percent of its local economy. That may be a little high, but it's not unreasonable for a near-coastal Florida county. What seem like big numbers might end up being negligible in both spending and effect when compared to the economy as a whole.

2. Make calculations per employee or per $1,000 spent

This exercise gets back to the idea that we can't think clearly about millions or billions of dollars – we need a "compared to what?" to begin to understand economic impact. Ask for the total number of jobs claimed and the total amount of money that is in question, either in tax abatements or direct subsidies.

There are three easy ways to evaluate those numbers. The first is to simply calculate the amount that is being paid to create a job. That will tell you right away whether the estimate is being done using a conservative or an expansive method.

The next is to compare it to the industry's revenue and job figures. . An easy rule of thumb is that an employer pays, in the costs of employment, about twice the salary or wages paid. But there's a big difference among industries in how much in sales it takes to support a single job. In 2010, for example, electric utilities took in $1 million for every job. Retailers only required $50,000. The Census has figures on revenue and employment by industry in its County Business Patterns series. Look to see whether the amount spent will be far more or less than the norm, and ask why.

The last relatively easy way is to see how long it will take to recover costs through increased tax revenues of newly employed people. Donald Barlett and James Steele did that calculation in 1998 for a shipyard in Pennsylvania, and found it would take about 50 years to pay back the state for its investment, but only if each worker earned $50,000 and all 950 of them were unemployed or came from outside the state.

WHO'S NO. 1? SCHOOL REPORTS, HEALTH CARE RANKINGS AND PLACES RATED – OPINIONS IN NUMBERS

Rankings cause no end of trouble in a newsroom. Whether we do them ourselves or publish those created by others, they still cause complaints. They're land mines in the news.

Readers and sources will complain that they're "just an opinion" and don't mean anything.

In health care, providers claim each patient is different, and you can't use numbers to rank them. In schools, it's every student. And in places, residents complain there's no way to account for all of the subtle differences between Miami and Seattle in a number.

These complaints are correct.

The indexes, whether they measure the "livability" of a place or the "quality" of a school, are just opinions.

Some are based on who is supposed to read the results – parents or teachers, employers or their employees. Others are based on what a survey says readers care about. Still others are based on common sense.

Don't be fooled by anyone who tells you it's purely by the numbers. They may use mathematical concepts to combine a series of measures. But underneath, they've constructed an index – or ranking system – that is based on an opinion of what's important, how it is best measured and how much it should count.

(Don't confuse these quality indexes with some that are done far more scientifically – the economic indexes you see each month or year like the Consumer Price Index and the Leading Economic Indicators. These are constructed using science. Generally, time series – indexes produced month after month – are done with more rigor than quality ratings.)

Each year, for example, a health care trade journal ranks each of the hospital companies in the U.S. These come out almost opposite the more famous ones constructed by U.S. News and World Report. The reason is that the trade journal cares about efficiency, and places a far greater weight on return to shareholders or profits. In writing about these, for instance, I've characterized them as the most profitable or efficient companies, not necessarily the "best."

Despite criticisms over its college and hospital rankings, U.S. News is still a good model. It attempts to use standards developed by the professions themselves. It uses measures that were developed for that purpose. And it tells us how it has compiled the ratings.

At the other end are the more qualitative rankings used to name great places to live or retire. Some refuse to provide formulas used, saying they're proprietary. Others change formulas each year to reflect what the current crop of readers/viewers/clients says is important to them.

REPORTING ON INDEXES AND RANKINGS

Although it can be complex, a source should be able to give you some basic information about how an index is constructed. Here's what to ask for:

A LIST OF EACH COMPONENT OF THE INDEX

The people who make an index should be able to provide you with a brief description of every element that went into it. It might include 100 items. That's fine. You'd rather have the list than not.

Sometimes the list is based on industry standards. For example, health care organizations were often rated on the national Healthy People 2010 program – a series of health care indicators that experts agreed were reasonable goals for the millennium.

Don't be frightened by some difficult concepts.

You might see the words "normalized" or "risk-adjusted" or some other fancy terms. These are ways to make the numbers behave – to compare one hospital to another when the patients have different ailments, or to make sure that a number will always be positive. You might also see some transformations to make sure that the number goes up as "quality" goes up. (Remember how percent changes don't move up and down the same way? They have to adjust for that problem.)

Just get the list and any formulas you can. If an adjusted or normalized score is important in the list, then ask how it's constructed. But usually they'll give you the formula – or a description of how it's derived – right with the list.

THE WEIGHTS WITH THE LIST

It doesn't help you to know what's in an index if you don't know how much importance it carries into the overall ranking. For example, schools might track how much money each teacher is paid, the attendance rate for a school or even the hours of volunteer work by parents. But if test scores make up three-quarters of the index, nothing else a school does will help its ranking much.

You might also ask how they came up with the weights. These are usually arbitrary – "Gee. I know test scores are twice as important as attendance, which in turn is twice as important as diversity to most parents."

Together, the list with its weights should make sense to you. You can often see the perspective of the organization making the index with these two lists. Ask how they came up with them, and ask about anything obvious that's missing.

ASK ABOUT MISSING VALUES

How does the ranking system account for missing information? Very rarely will every piece of data be available for every school, hospital, or city. As a result, the makers have to decide what to do instead. Here are the choices:

1. Assign either all of the points or none of the points. Both of these can be unfair. Sometimes the makers will assign zero if the institution refuses to divulge the information, but some other method if it can't, like a school that doesn't have fifth-graders.

2. Assign the average for all others reporting that item. If there's no fifth grade, then, the makers might assign the average score for all other fifth grades.

3. Remove the weight, making the index more dependent on what the institution can give them. This is most common. The drawback on this method is that it encourages the institutions to only divulge the measures on which they score well, letting you depend only on them.

HOW IS IT AGGREGATED (COMBINED)?

There are a few different ways to come up with the rankings. Many places will use some combination of these methods. In general, they must come up with something that isn't sensitive to the unit of measure that each item carries. For example, you can't combine teacher salaries with test scores to come up with any meaningful number unless they're on the same scale. Here are a few methods commonly used:

RANKINGS: Each item is ranked within the list of companies or schools or cities, then the ranks are added up.

The disadvantage of this method is that schools with almost the same performance can come out ranked very differently. It's not sensitive to how much difference there is in the measure, only the rank of each item. The advantage is the opposite: There's always a winner. It's also easy to construct.

POINT COUNTS: An index will often add to 100 points, reminding you of the tests you got in school.

These points are doled out to individual items, much like your grades in school were doled out to the final exam, the mid-term and class participation.

Make sure that if you have a system like this, you know how the points are allocated within a group as well as when they get combined. For example, does a school get 10 of 10 points for meeting a certain standard, or is it determined by a ranking?

STANDARD SCORES: One of the most common standard scores you see in life is the SAT. The makers use a mathematical formula that will always come out to 200 to 800 points. Then you can make an average of these.

Any number can be forced into this scale. It's a combination of rankings and point counts in that it is still sensitive to how much difference there is between the schools or hospitals, but is still relative – it's measured against an average. These are sometimes called normed scores.

HOW STABLE IS THE INDEX?

In life, change happens slowly.

When index makers have been around for a while, you can test a current number against previous numbers to look for problems.

For example, one of the annual city rankings is quite unstable. A city can rank No. 1 in one year's ranking, and 105th the next. Part of this comes from poor data. If the inputs aren't stable, the index won't be, either. Part of it comes from tinkering around with the formula each year. Make sure you know what's causing it.

CHAPTER 5:
Surveys and Polls – Numbers as summaries and guesses

There are wonderful books available for reporters on deconstructing polls and surveys. But no book on using math in the newsroom would be complete without addressing this issue.

The key failure in reporting on polls and surveys is ignoring what we know. The mismatch between what a headline or story says, and what a graphic shows, is often the item that prompts critics to question our understanding of basic statistics and math.

KNOW YOUR POLLSTER

One easy way to know whether a survey is legitimate is to evaluate the group doing the research. This isn't always as easy as it seems, since special interest groups can hire reputable pollsters for their work.

But most professional pollsters have standards. Gallup, Roper, Mason Dixon and many news organizations' polling operations aren't willing to risk their credibility on a small survey for a special interest group. You can take some comfort when one of these companies is in the mix.

One way to find out whether a poll is conducted by a generally reputable group is to check its history in the Roper Center for Public Opinion's database of past survey questions. If it's missing, it doesn't mean much, since not all pollsters participate. But if it's there, it might help you.

Beware of polls sponsored or conducted by candidates, special interest groups and companies with an obvious interest in the outcome. Ask who paid for the poll.

There are a few things that come from using a reputable pollster:

1.STANDARD SAMPLING TECHNIQUES.
Pollsters match the way they choose people with the goals of the survey. They may sample 350 people, 500 people or more than 1,000 people, depending on the ways they want to break down the answers. They might also "oversample" some groups of people that rarely answer polls: young people, men or Northerners. Using a reputable pollster removes much of your concern regarding proper selection techniques.

2.CAUTIOUS REPORTING OF RESULTS.
Good pollsters will refuse to break down a survey into such small groups as to be meaningless. For example, you may ask them how 20 to 25-year-olds answered, and they may tell you, "We won't do that." It's because they know their samples can't support such details. This is good, not bad. Don't force a reputable pollster to go beyond the scope of the survey.

3.TIME-TESTED QUESTIONS.
Minor differences in questions can lead to wildly different responses. Studies have shown that one word in a question on past voting habits can significantly change a pollster's estimate of who is likely to vote. Professional pollsters watch these questions and apply their experience to the wording.

QUESTION WORDING AND SEQUENCE

Ask for the exact question wording. Better yet, ask for the full list of questions (or at least the relevant section) to see where in the list it falls. Look for:

CLARITY. If you stumble over the questions, so did the respondents.

DOUBLE-BARRELED QUESTIONS. Just like a reporter in an interview, a pollster can ask two questions at once. Unlike the reporter, the pollster allows only one answer: "Do you favor or oppose health care reform and strict price controls?"

LOADED QUESTIONS. Rarely found among reputable pollsters, but rampant in special interest groups. Some are obvious: "Do you favor or oppose the president's health care proposal, which will lead to lower costs?" Some are less obvious: "Did you vote in the last presidential election?" Ask how you would answer.

CAN RESPONDENTS POSSIBLY ANSWER THE QUESTION? Whenever there's a big news event, pollsters ask what the effect will be. Will there be another terrorist attack on U.S. soil? Will there be peace in the Middle East? Although these questions might help you figure out whether the public approves or disapproves of a policy, it tells you nothing else of meaning; the vast majority couldn't possibly know.

WOULD YOU LIE IF ASKED? I live in the Washington, D.C., area. Here, it's a point of pride to live close to the city. So the median commuting time recorded by the U.S. Census for my ZIP code is 20 minutes. But if I want to get somewhere on time, I really have to leave an hour early to account for subway delays or traffic. It should take 20 minutes. It rarely does.

LOOK ALSO FOR THE SEQUENCE OF QUESTIONS. An abortion question that follows one asking about euthanasia might prompt one response. The same question following one on women's rights might prompt a very different response. Ask how they determined the order of the questions.

NOTE: This list was adapted from the "Newsroom Guide to Polls and Surveys," by G. Cleveland Wilhoit and David H. Weaver.

SAMPLING METHOD AND RESPONSE RATES

You don't need a lot of respondents to produce a good survey. Instead, you need a few different characteristics to produce one.

1. SELECTION TECHNIQUE

To represent a bigger group, a survey must be selected so that everyone it represents has an equal chance of selection. This isn't necessarily a "pure random sample," but many of the same characteristics apply. In general, statisticians require some form of randomness. They must start with a full list of all the people they want to represent. This is usually done by random-digit dialing–it gives every residential phone number a chance of selection.

2. RESPONSE RATES

Telephone surveys often produce response rates of about 60 percent to 70 percent. That means that many people refuse to talk to a pollster. It doesn't really matter, so long as there's nothing about the people who refuse to talk that makes them different from others.

For example, if many Hispanic respondents can't answer polls given in English, then any poll that affects the Latin community might be biased toward English-speaking residents. If young people are out when pollsters call more often than older people, they will be under-represented in the answer.

Ask your pollster about response rates, and whether there might be a bias in who answered.

THE MARGIN OF ERROR (SAMPLING ERROR)

We often publish margins of error, or sampling errors, right in our stories or graphics. Then we promptly ignore them in both the story and the headline. Don't do this.

Margins of error tell you how confident a pollster is that its answer is correct. A 2.5 percent margin of error means that it will quote answers in a 5 percentage point range.

EXAMPLE:

In a poll, 45 percent of the respondents said they would vote for Mayor Jones, beating Commissioner Smith who got 40 percent. Fifteen percent were undecided. The margin of error is ±3 percent. This means that the real answer for Jones is somewhere between 42 and 48 percent; the real answer for Smith is somewhere between 37 and 43 percent.

You don't know who would win if the election were conducted today. There's a good chance that Smith is actually beating Jones, 43 percent to 42 percent. There's a small chance (usually 5 percent) that the error in the poll is even bigger.

THE ELEMENTS OF SAMPLING ERROR

There are three elements in a margin of error:

1. THE NUMBER OF PEOPLE IN THE SURVEY. The minimum is usually around 385 responses. Many national polls are quite adequate using a survey of only about 1,500 people.

However, you need to use the margin of error on the total of any group, not the total of the entire survey. So if there are only 50 answers among black people, your poll is inadequate to distinguish the differences in opinions among African Americans.

2. THE DIFFERENCES IN THE ANSWERS.

There's a smaller margin of error when 90 percent of the people respond one way than when 55 percent respond that way.

Many companies don't worry about this: They report the most conservative possible estimate of margin of error – the one that would be calculated if all answers were 50-50. The reason is that they can then report one figure for the entire survey, not individual questions and their answers.

If your survey has one number in it, you might ask whether it's a conservative estimate or an aggressive one, or on which response it's based. You can also be more confident of questions with a big spread than a little one.

3. HOW ACCURATE THEY WANT THE ANSWERS TO BE

Generally, pollsters use a "95 percent confidence interval". This means they're willing to accept the notion that one of every 20 polls will be wrong beyond the margin of error.

CALCULATING YOUR OWN MARGIN OF ERROR

Pollsters can use a complex calculation to account for odd sample designs and other technical problems. You won't always be able to replicate it. But you can check the basics with a simple calculation that often comes out the same as the more rigorous calculations. If yours are slightly different than the pollster's, don't worry about it. If they're very different (say, more than a percentage point), then ask how it was derived.

Here is the formula:

$$1.96 \times \sqrt{\frac{\text{Yes} \times \text{No}}{\text{\# answers}}}$$

The 1.96 is used when you want a 95 percent confidence interval. It means you're willing to accept the risk that one of 20 polls is wrong, beyond the margin of error. Increase this number to 3.0 if you want to be 99 percent sure that your answer is within the margin of error.

"Yes" is the proportion (or percent / 100) of people who answered "Yes," or one way. "No" is the proportion of people who answered "No", or any other way.

Here are three examples:

EXAMPLE 1:	In a poll, 535 Missourians answered questions about health insurance. Ten percent said they had none. The other 90 percent gave the type of insurance they had, or said they didn't know.
	For this specific question, the margin of error is close to:
	Step 1: Yes x No = 0.9 x 0.1 = 0.09
	Step 2: (Yes x No) / number of answers = 0.09 / 535 = (a big long answer with an e in it on your calculator or spreadsheet, which corresponds to about 0.000168)
	Step 3: The square root of that number = 0.01297
	Step 4: Multiply by 1.96 = 0.0254, or ±2.5 percent. So, based on the power of your poll, you're pretty sure that between 7.5 and 12.5 percent of Missourians lack insurance.
	Because of the nature of this story, you might prefer to use this estimate to the more conservative measures in a survey like this one. Sometimes, statisticians can be too conservative when they report their answers, especially if they don't want you to quote them.

EXAMPLE 2:	Another calculation with the same results. This time, you want to give the most conservative answer for the entire poll, not just this answer in this question. This is the most common way to do these estimates.
	Step 1: Instead of yes x no, we'll use a 50-50 split:
	Yes X No = 0.5 x 0.5 = 0.25 (This is where the conservatism comes in)
	Step 2: (Yes x No) / # Answers = 0.25 / 535 = 0.000467
	Step 3: The square root of that number = 0.0216
	Step 4: Multiply by 1.96 = .042 or ±4.2 percentage points. Here, you'd express the answer as somewhere between about 6 and 14 percent of the people without health insurance.

EXAMPLE 3:	Sticking with the conservative estimate, you want to be more confident that the answer you get is the real answer, leaving only a 1 in 100 chance that the range is too narrow.

Step 1: Yes x No = 0.5 x 0.5 = 0.25

Step 2: (Yes x No) / # Answers = 0.25 / 535 = 0.000467

Step 3: The square root of that number = 0.0216

Step 4: Instead of 1.96, multiply by 3.0 (this is where the better confidence comes in):, = .065 or ±6.5 percent. Now, with a little more confidence, you know that somewhere between 3.5 and 16.5 percent of Missourians lack insurance. This level of confidence, however, is rarely used in polls.

SAMPLE SIZES AND THEIR CONSERVATIVE MARGINS OF ERROR

One thing that often trips up beginners is that the number of people you're describing is irrelevant. It doesn't matter if you're measuring the mood of the country or the mood of the city. The sample sizes required are the same.

(There is, however, an adjustment pollsters can make when they've actually surveyed a big percentage of the population. You'll rarely see it.)

The biggest thing to remember is that with too small a sample, you won't be able to measure a difference in opinion even if there is one. With a very large sample, you'll measure a "statistically significant" difference, even if it's trivial.

SAMPLE SIZE	CONFIDENCE	
	95%	99%
385	5.0	7.6
500	4.4	6.7
750	3.6	5.5
1,000	3.1	4.7
1,500	2.5	3.9
3,500	1.7	2.5

This chart shows you why so many national polls are about 1,500 people – it's the number needed to reduce the margin of error to plus or minus 2.5 percentage points.

MORE POLL AND SURVEY TIPS

- "Don't know," or "No opinion," are answers. Especially in campaigns, the number of undecideds can be even more important than the number who have decided.

- Don't get frightened by seemingly small sample sizes. Instead, examine the margin of error. A thousand responses are adequate for most polls, so long as the answers aren't broken into small subgroups. A typical size is between 350 and 400 respondents for a local poll.

  In recent years, the identification of likely voters has become one of the most difficult issues in polling. Many of the differences among the polls in national elections hinge on that decision.

- Consider skipping a story on a poll or survey in which the sponsor will not give you the sample size, sampling method, response rate, margin of error, confidence interval or exact question wording. Your ability to get at least some of those items tells you the pollster is serious.

- Make sure your story doesn't revolve around meaningless differences or changes. A difference isn't "significant" unless it's greater than twice the margin of error.

- Polls can be wrong! The margin of error, say ±3 percentage points, tells you there's a 95 percent chance the true answer is within 6 percentage points (or, say, 41 percent to 47 percent.) That means there's a 5 percent chance it's even more than that, and then all bets are off. If a poll tells you something you can't believe, consider not believing it!

CHAPTER 6:

The 10 most wanted list: Mistakes in the news from simple math to lapses in judgment

So far, I've focused on what, as journalists, we can do right in reporting on numbers and working with them in the newsroom. But like others who write on the subject, it's difficult to avoid the common mistakes that find their way into the paper or onto the air.

Here is my 10 Most Wanted List:

NO. 10. FLIPPED PROBABILITIES AND THE CANCER CLUSTER

I call a flipped probability one that has been generated backward.

It may be quite true to say that finding a group of seven cancer cases in a building is one in a billion. But it may also be true that finding a group of seven cases in *any* building in the world is pretty even odds.

This is a difficult concept, and is most easily translated by using an example from the state lottery. If the state sells 60 million tickets out of 80 million possible combinations of numbers, the probability that you'll win is one out of 80 million. But the probability of *anyone* winning is 60 million out of 80 million, or 75 percent.

In other words, you're pretty sure someone will win, you just can't say in advance who will win. The same principle applies to cancer and lightning strikes. We know that you're not very likely to get cancer this year. We also know that someone in your ZIP code probably will.

To figure out whether a rare event is actually unexpected, you usually have to figure out the probability of it *not* happening *anywhere* rather than the probability of it *happening somewhere*. This can be difficult, but there are computer programs to help you with it. Get the help of a good statistician or epidemiologist before quoting rare probabilities.

NO. 9. THE MAGIC RUBBER BAND, OR MISUNDERSTANDING

"THE LAW OF AVERAGES"

Imagining a magic rubber band that automatically snaps back to place is one of the biggest errors in mathematical thinking in the newsroom. In fact, we'll often hear the phrase, "the law of averages", and think this is what it means. Mathematicians call this the gambler's fallacy. It's the idea that the dice must roll your way next time because it's time – they've been rolling against you for too long.

Instead, the concept – called "regression to the mean" – is that an unusual event is expected to be followed by a usual event. The best description I've seen of this phenomenon is in *Speaking of Journalism*, a collection by William Zinsser. In it, science writer

Kevin McKean describes a story about a psychologist working with flight instructors.

One of these instructors couldn't believe the studies showing that reward works better than punishment to improve performance. After all, the instructor said, whenever he praised pilots for a beautifully executed maneuver, they did worse the next time out. But when he punished pilots for sloppy work, they did better.

The answer is the regression to the mean: When events have some random element to them, an extraordinary event is usually followed by an ordinary one. So the unusually perfect maneuver is often followed by a more common one. So is an atrociously sloppy one.

NO. 8. OVERCOOKING VEGETABLES WITH AN AVERAGE OF AN AVERAGE

You usually can't just average a bunch of averages and come up with anything of meaning. Stay away from this technique. It will not only be misleading, it will be wrong.

It's like overcooking a vegetable medley – you can't really taste any of the flavors and you're not sure what you're eating when you're done. Although there are exceptions to the rule, you'll usually want to weight averages or come up with a different technique.

Sometimes, reporters take a bunch of percent changes, say, in a budget, and compute an average for the "average percent change." This treats the 140 percent increase in a new, small department the same as the 2 percent increase for education.

See the section on averages in Chapter 2 for more details.

NO. 7. WHO CARES? OR LOSING SIGHT OF YOUR BASE

Small numbers generate big percentages. Big numbers generate small percentages. That means that keeping track of the actual number of deaths, arrests, crimes or any other figure is just as important as quoting its rate or its rate of change.

As a rule of thumb, it's difficult to quote a percentage when you're working with fewer than 100 items – people, dollars or homes. That's because a change in each represents more than one percentage point. Revert to raw numbers – 1 out of 12 – if you want to put perspective into that story. If nothing else, round off a lot, so you're describing "more than half" or "almost two-thirds."

NO. 6. FALSE PRECISION

Beyond any other generalization, numbers are guesses. They're also out of date the minute they're collected.

This doesn't suggest we should avoid using the numbers available to us. But we should also take many with a grain of salt. That means avoiding the false precision that's often implied in our stories.

You can check whether you're relying on false precision by rounding off every decimal point in your story before it runs.

Some news organizations have style rules that require keeping the decimal places. You might have to. But take another look if your story depends on the decimal places to make its point.

These little numbers may actually mean something, especially if you're dealing with rates like unemployment or crime. And we've already seen how changing the base can make a little number into a big one. So if they're accurate, fine.

But they often aren't accurate to the level of detail that the story implies. Instead, they're sometimes based on small samples, rounded numbers and guesses of all kinds.

An example can be seen by using the inflation-adjusted estimates we computed earlier in this book. Using one version of the CPI, we'd come up with an inflation-adjusted teacher salary of $53,234. Using a version of the CPI calculated with the exact same inputs, but expressed on a different scale, the answer is $53,226. They're off by $8. The answer still rounds off to $53,200.

Don't depend on meaningless differences in numbers for your story. They'll be challenged, and the challengers will be right.

NO. 5. THE IF... THEN DISEASE: CONFUSING CAUSE AND EFFECT

Critics often overstate the extent to which reporters confuse correlation with causality. But it's worth repeating because so many critics believe that reporters don't understand the difference between correlation – two things somehow connected with each other – and causality – the reason for the connection, which is the thing we all care about.

Correlation is a mathematical concept. If one thing – say, poverty – rises, and another – say, test scores – fall, they are correlated. That is, you can predict scores when you know a student's wealth. You can also predict wealth when you know a student's scores.

There are all kinds of examples of the confusion between correlation and causation used in textbooks, which have little application in journalism. One, for example, is the link between the number of clergymen in a city and the number of bottles of liquor sold. Of course, there is a missing link: the number of people in each city.

In "Statistics: A Spectator Sport," author Richard M. Jaeger tells us a little about the ways researchers decide whether they've found a cause and effect.

a. DOES THE CAUSE COME BEFORE THE EFFECT?

This seems more obvious than it sometimes is. Test scores may depend on the number of teachers in a classroom. Spending may, in turn, depend on performance just last year. Performance in a school doesn't usually change that quickly.

b. IS THERE A THIRD EVENT THAT CAUSES THE RELATIONSHIP?

Again, a school example is worth noting. Most reporters would find that high minority populations in schools are associated with low test scores. But a third factor – poverty and education of the parents – play a role in both the cause and effect in this case. Although someone's ethnicity comes before just about anything else, few would argue they cause any of the difficulties minorities face in school.

c. IS THERE ANOTHER EXPLANATION?

Can you think up – or can someone else think up – rival theories that are equally sound? Look to your reporting effort rather than statistics for this step.

d. DOES ANYTHING REFUTE THE THEORY?

Are there other studies that fail to show the expected causal relationship? Why might your theory work locally but fail elsewhere? Why might it seem sound one year but fall apart in another?

NO. 4. IGNORING THE LITTLE VOICE INSIDE YOU

Reporters sometimes take a number at face value, ignoring everything else they know to be true. This happens most frequently with polls, which can be wrong. Put every number you see into what one author calls a "crap detector." If it doesn't stand up to common sense, or if what you know contradicts it, it might actually be wrong.

NO. 3. INADEQUATE SOURCING

I'll admit it. I've been desperate at times to find a number – any number – to satisfy an editor who wants to put a story in perspective.

But we're often willing to accept shoddy numbers because we're uncomfortable challenging the source who spouts them. Or because they're boring, and you're ready to get to the story, not the study. Or they're alarming, and that makes for better copy.

In the early 1990s, a number was thrown around by the Clinton administration, labor experts and others who were lamenting the new lack of corporate loyalty. Each quoted the same figure – that workers were now expected to change careers six times in their working lives. Like others, I was assigned a story on the topic, and sought as part of it to find the source of the number. It turned out to be a weak study on a different subject. But the number had become part of the folklore.

Don't just say "phew" when you get the number you need for the story. Ask the source, "how do you know? What's the reference?" Then put it to a gut-test and seek out the original source.

NO. 2. PACKING NUMBERS INTO A STORY

One of our biggest mistakes is to try to quote too many numbers, rather than selecting the ones that tell the story best. I think this is done in the spirit of fairness – if each number is an opinion, then we need to balance them.

But now that you're more comfortable with the art of using numbers well, consider reducing the digits in your copy substantially. As William Blundell wrote, packing numbers into a story is probably the demon that leads to more unread prose than any other. Don't let it happen to you.

NO. 1. LETTING 10-2 PARALYZE US

Especially in medical and education reporting, we'll let the problems with numbers and our understanding of them reduce us to stenographers.

I hope that the rest of this book has given you a little confidence to read the reports that the experts write, rather than just quote their press releases. And I hope you've come to the understanding that numbers are just another way to express an opinion, a summary or a story. If you've come away with anything else, I hope you've come away with the idea that much of working with numbers and research is just common sense. Use it.

CHAPTER 7:
Lotteries, lightning strikes and longevity – a note on probabilities

Most math books, notably those by John Allen Paulos, focus on probability theory – the idea that you can predict the chances that an event will happen using its historical trends or a known quantity. Probability comes up rarely in news, so this section will be brief. But it's worth understanding how probability works and how you can troubleshoot some of the probabilities you see in the news.

CALCULATING A PROBABILITY

To calculate any probability, you'll use a simple ratio.

Here are some examples:

LIGHTNING STRIKES	In the Tampa Bay area, about 20 people a year are hit by lightning. About 4.3 million live in the area. So the probability of getting hit by lightning in any given year is 20 / 4,300,000, or 0.000005. That's a hard number to talk about. So most people would simplify it by talking about "one out of" something. To get that "something," divide 1 by your answer: 1 / .000005 = 200,000 So the probability of being hit by lightning is one out of 200,000.

DYING OF CANCER

Cancer death rates are age-specific, so let's just choose an age as an example. In 2009, for instance, there were about 6,000 deaths of women 45 to 54-year-old women attributed to breast cancer. There were 22.6 million women in that age group nationally.

To get the death rate, divide the number of people who died of the cancer by the number of people in the age group:

6,000/22,600,000 = .000265

This number is also called the "probability" of dying of breast cancer as a woman between the ages of 45 and 54. (A probability is a proportion, and is always between 0 (no chance) and 1 (certainty)).

To get a death rate, multiply by 100,000:

.0000265 x 100,000 = 26.5, or a rate of about 27 per 100,000 women.

Some people prefer to say it more simply. If you divide 1 by your probability, you can get a sentence that's much easier on your readers:

1/.000265 = 3,774.

This means that women in this age group have about a one in 3,800 chance of dying of breast cancer.

Most of the time, probabilities of dying are expressed in terms of annual risk. Be careful with lifetime risks. They're much trickier and depend on whether you assume someone will live to a certain age.

LOTTERIES

Helpful lottery officials print the odds of winning a game on the back of the ticket. This section will show how they compute those odds.

Lottery odds are based on "combinatorics," which is a branch of mathematics that counts things. It's the factorials, combinations and permutations that convinced many of us, somewhere around fifth grade, that we didn't want anything to do with math.

To figure out the number of possible lottery numbers that can be picked, you need to know what numbers are allowed and how many numbers are allowed.

The chances of winning a lottery are always 1 out of the number of possible number combinations in the lottery ticket. So if there are 2 million possible tickets, your chances are 1 out of 2 million.

Note that there's no rubber band here. The chances of winning are exactly the same from one number to the next and from one lottery to the next. Just because a number has been picked before doesn't mean it won't be picked again. The number itself, barring fraud or cheating, is irrelevant in the calculation of the odds or probabilities.

FIGURING LOTTERY ODDS	A typical example, this one drawn from "200% of Nothing," uses a Pick 6 lottery in which you can choose six numbers ranging from 1 to 36. You're not allowed to repeat numbers, and the order they appear in the ticket doesn't matter.

For the first number, you can pick any of the 36 numbers. But there are only 35 numbers left to choose from when you get to the second. And 34 left after that. In other words, for every 36 ways to choose the first number, there are 35 ways to choose the second number.

When you see the words, "for every," you should think about multiplication:

36 x 35 x 34 x 33 x 32 x 31 = # of total combinations of 36 numbers in six picks.

But there's a problem. It double-counts lots of the combinations, because it treats 1, 17, 27, 2, 18, 30 as a different combination of 18, 2, 17, 30, 27, 1. We, however, don't care what order you pick them in, only what numbers appear on the lottery ticket.

So we'll reduce this number by dividing it by:

6 x 5 x 4 x 3 x 2 x 1

because there are six ways to pick the first number, five ways to pick the second, etc.

The final answer is:

(36 x 35 x 34 x 33 x 32 x 31) / (6 x 5 x 4 x 3 x 2 x 1)

OR 1,402,410,240 / 720 = 1,947,792 possible tickets. |

ANOTHER EXAMPLE OF COMBINATIONS	You can use this concept whenever you're trying to figure out how many possible events could occur.
	One Friday evening, for example, a reporter called IRE's database library with a question: How could he figure out the number of simultaneous decisions a baseball manager makes when he fields a team? In other words, how many combinations of nine players can be made out of a roster of 25?
	It's the same idea:
	$(25 \times 24 \times 23 \times 22 \times 21 \times 20 \times 19 \times 18 \times 17) / (9 \times 8 \times 7 \times 6 \times 5 \times 4 \times 3 \times 2 \times 1)$.
	You can do the math. But it comes out to more than 2 million possible combinations of the players without regard to position. (If you want to count every possible position as a separate combination, you'd skip the division, and come up with about 740 million possible answers.) The lesson is that simple combinations of numbers can grow very quickly to huge numbers through this multiplication.

TIP FOR SPREADSHEET USERS

Excel has some handy functions to help you with this. It figures out the calculation we just made by using the function, COMBIN(# of possible numbers, # you'll pick). So for the baseball example, it would be COMBIN(25, 9) or the lottery would be COMBIN(36,6).

If you want it to keep the double-counting of equivalent lottery numbers, then use PERMUT(# of possible numbers, # you'll pick). And if you want it to do the calculation we did as our denominator, the simple factorial, then use FACT(#).

SMALL PROBABILITIES X BIG NUMBERS = BIG MISTAKES

In statistics, big numbers generate big numbers even in small percentages. The classic examples arise in drug testing and expert testimony in court.

We'll take the drug testing problem as the easier one to see. But remember that if you're covering a case, and an expert talks about one-in-a-gazillion chances of something happening, it matters how many gazillions there are out there.

Here's the example you'll find in many other books on the topic of math:

A large company has 5,000 employees and plans to test all of them for drug use. About 10 percent of the employees actually use drugs, and the test is what's commonly called 98 percent accurate – 98 percent of the positives are really drug users, and 98 percent of the negatives really don't use drugs.

With numbers like this, the chances are about one in five that a person who tests positive is actually drug-free.

1. Of 5,000 people, 4,500 are drug-free. The test correctly guesses that 4410 are drug-free. It incorrectly guesses the other 90 are users.

2. Of the 5,000 people, 500 use drugs. The test correctly guesses that 490 use drugs and that 10 don't.

3. The chance of being drug free when you test positive: 90 / (490+90) = .18, or almost one-fifth.

COINCIDENCES OVER TIME – COMBINING PROBABILITIES

Big coincidences are news. There's nothing wrong with treating them as such. This is one disagreement I have with the experts who say we should ignore coincidences until they're proven to be something more than that.

It's useful, though, if we know just how much of a coincidence it really is.

To get a probability over time, you multiply each probability together. But you have to be careful – sometimes you don't care when or where an event could happen, only that it might happen at all.

STOCK PICKERS

One premise of betting on the stock market is that all of the information there is to know is available to anyone with the time and energy to review it. Prices for stocks are supposedly the collective wisdom of the marketplace. So there should be no advantage to anyone, other than a better way to understand that wisdom.

When a fund manager outpaces the market for five years in a row, we often write about his strategy and his unusual insights. It could, however, be dumb luck.

Start with the proposition that it's luck whether you outpace the market in a given year: The probability of winning a year is 0.5, or 1 in 2, or 50 percent.

In the first year, 50 of a group of 100 fund managers are expected to outpace the market; 50 won't.

Next, take the following year: 50 percent of each group will outpace the market, making 25 who have done it two years in a row. Now 50 percent the following year, to 12.5 percent. And 50 percent of the next two years, or 3 percent

So dumb luck would suggest you'd find 3 of these 100 gurus who outpace the market for five years running.

BATTING STREAKS

In baseball, 1998 was the year of the batting streak. Mark McGwire and Sammy Sosa smashed longstanding home run records.

But each year, local reporters focus on smaller streaks: 5 games in a row with home runs or 10 games running without any home runs.

To keep the numbers simple, let's say a player hits 35 home runs out of 140 games. That means he's expected to hit 0.25 home runs each game, or one home run out of every four games.

Let's do the simple one first: The chances of his hitting a home run in 10 consecutive games. This one's simple multiplication: 0.25 times itself 10 times, for a probability of one in more than a million.

But the opposite isn't true. It's much more common to go 10 games without a home run at all.

To do this calculation, you have to figure out the chances of not hitting a home run in consecutive games. That's because you don't care which game he hits one in. It only matters that he hasn't hit any.

In the first game, his chances are .75, or three in four that he won't. In the second, it's .75 x .75 that he won't. And so on, until you multiply .75 by itself 10 times, for a chance of 0.05, or one in 20 that he'll come up dry in all 10 games.

CANCER CLUSTERS

I've saved cancer clusters for last because it's the same idea as the cold streak.

But before you go any further, say this out loud: I won't find a cancer cluster. I won't find a cancer cluster. I won't find a cancer cluster.

You might, however, find a bunch of cancer cases in the same place. It's not the same thing. Documenting a cancer cluster is really hard work, and the experts usually don't try unless they start with the following elements:

- Knowledge about everyone in the group who was exposed to the suspected carcinogen. That means that you have to know about the people exposed, not the people who got sick.

- The type of cancer ought to be similar, or known to be caused by similar things. You'd be hard-pressed to document a cancer cluster that contained a mix of breast cancer and childhood leukemia.

- There ought to be strong medical reasons to believe that the cancer is caused by something to which people were exposed. It's not enough to know that leukemia erupted around a toxic waste dump. Instead, there ought to be something in the waste that is a carcinogen.

- The rates of cancer are significantly higher than you'd expect from a population that size.

Most of these elements are very difficult for reporters to prove. A reading of "A Civil Action" shows how hard it is to prove.

We usually are only prepared to write about the last of the elements: Whether the incidence of the cancer is higher than you'd expect. Most of the time, this is calculated much like the relative risk calculation earlier in this booklet. Statisticians will use a probability test to figure out if that difference is likely to happen by chance.

But they also look at another calculation: The chances that a town like Woburn, Mass., would never have that many cancer cases together. It's based on a probability distribution worked out eons ago and what statisticians call "life table analysis." There are computer programs developed to do these calculations. But it's based on the same idea as the losing streak. Instead of figuring out the chances that Woburn would have 25 cases of childhood leukemia, they would figure out the chances that any town its size would have that many cases. Make sure you understand which they mean.

CHAPTER 8:
Other resources

AT IRE

Investigative Reporters & Editors along with the National Institute for Computer-Assisted Reporting can provide a number of resources that are helpful to reporters dealing with numbers.

TRAINING

BOOT CAMPS

Along with its regular computer-assisted reporting boot camps, where journalists are taught to use spreadsheets, databases and Internet resources, IRE offers an Advanced Boot Camp on Statistics annually for reporters who want to move beyond basic CAR and use statistical analysis in their work.

NEWSROOM TRAINING

IRE can parachute into your news organization, bringing laptop computers, stories from its vast archives and time-tested techniques for training in everything from basic CAR to statistical analysis, mapping and advanced data techniques.

PRACTICE DATA SETS

Data sets are provided for those who have already taken training and want to stay practiced between CAR assignments. Includes slices of data for Excel, Access, FoxPro and SPSS.

RESOURCE CENTER

STORIES AND TIPSHEETS

The IRE resource center (http://ire.org/resource-center/) is a major research library containing over 26,000 investigative stories – print, broadcast and online. Add to that more than 4,000 tipsheets gathered from speakers at IRE's national conferences, and you have a treasure trove of information you can use to jump start your stories. The stories and tipsheets are searchable over the Web.

DATABASE LIBRARY

IRE, along with the National Institute for Computer-Assisted Reporting, maintains a library of constantly updated government data sets. Journalists can usually buy whole databases or state slices of cleaned and formatted data useful in any number of stories. Examples include crime statistics, aviation data, highway accidents and federal contracts to private companies. The analysts working in the library can often help you with your "numbers questions."

PUBLICATIONS

UPLINK

Uplink is the online magazine of the National Institute for Computer-Assisted Reporting. It's a place where reporters share their experiences in using databases, spreadsheets, statistics, mapping and other CAR techniques. Subscription information can be found at http://ire.org/blog/uplink/

THE IRE JOURNAL

The IRE Journal is the quarterly magazine of Investigative Reporters & Editors, Inc. IRE members receive the magazine at no extra charge, or it can subscribed to by non-members. The Journal includes articles by reporters who have used investigative techniques to develop story packages and projects for their newsrooms. Resources are often listed to assist others in doing similar stories.

BEAT BOOK SERIES

The book you are reading now is part of a series of reporter guides, often focused on specific reporting niches where numbers are involved.

MAILING LISTS

NICAR-L and Census-L are listservs where journalists help each other with numbers questions – often on deadline. Subscribe by visiting http://www.ire.org/resource-center/listservs/ on the IRE site.

THE WEB

The Web has meant easier access to math and statistics resources for reporters – especially on deadline. While IRE can't vouch for every site out there when you find yourself stumped, we have compiled a short list of great places to start.

www.census.gov/popest

The Census Bureau's population estimates for the United States, areas within the United States and Puerto Rico. These are good numbers with which to practice.

www.robertniles.com

A great site for basic math questions, how-to conversions, and has links to stats.

https://www.cia.gov/library/publications/the-world-factbook/appendix/appendix-g.html

Weights and measure conversions, including conversion factors on an astounding number of units. Brought to you by the CIA's World Factbook.

FRACTIONS AND PERCENTAGES – CONVERSION CHART

Fraction	It's the same as	Or in words	Percent	Easier words for readers
1/10		1 of 10	10%	A tenth
1/9		1 of 9	11%	A ninth
1/8		1 of 8	13%	An eighth
1/7		1 of 7	14%	A seventh
1/6		1 of 6	17%	A sixth
1/5	2/10	1 of 5	20%	A fifth
2/9		2 of 9	22%	Almost a quarter
1/4	2/8	1 of 4	25%	A quarter
2/7		2 of 7	29%	More than a quarter
3/10		3 of 10	30%	Nearly a third
1/3	2/6, 3/9	1 of 3	33%	A third
3/8		3 of 8	38%	More than a third
2/5	4/10	2 of 5	40%	
3/7		3 of 7	43%	
4/9		4 of 9	44%	Almost half
1/2	5/10;4/8; 3/6;2/4	1 of 2	50%	Half
5/9		5 of 9	56%	More than half
4/7		4 of 7	57%	More than half
3/5	6/10	3 of 5	60%	
5/8		5 of 8	63%	Almost two-thirds
2/3	4/6,6/96/8	2 of 3	67%	Two-thirds
7/10		7 of 10	70%	
5/7		5 of 7	71%	
3/4		3 of 4	75%	Three-quarters
7/9		7 of 9	78%	More than three quarters
4/5	8/10	4 of 5	80%	
5/6		5 of 6	83%	
6/7		6 of 7	85%	
7/8		7 of 8	88%	
8/9		8 of 9	89%	
9/10		9 of 10	90%	
1			100%	As much as; all
2			200%	Double
3			300%	Triple

ABOUT THE AUTHOR

Sarah Cohen is the editor of computer-assisted reporting at The New York Times. She previously served as the Knight professor of computational journalism at Duke University and as a database editor at the Washington Post. She has shared in the Pulitzer Prize for investigative reporting, the Goldsmith award and the IRE medal. She also has worked as a reporter in Florida and as IRE's training director from 1996 to 1998. She has served on the IRE board of directors since 2010.

IRE BOARD OF DIRECTORS (2014)

David Cay Johnston, Syracuse University . . . . President
Sarah Cohen, New York Times . . . . Vice President
Ellen Gabler, Milwaukee Journal Sentinel . . . . Secretary
Andrew Donohue, The Center for Investigative Reporting . . . Treasurer
Mc Nelly Torres, NBC Miami . . . . Executive Member
Ziva Branstetter, Tulsa World
Robert Cribb, Toronto Star
Leonard Downie Jr., The Washington Post/Arizona State University
Manny Garcia, Naples Daily News
Matt Goldberg, NBC Bay Area
Josh Meyer, Medill National Security Journalism Initiative
T. Christian Miller, ProPublica
Stuart Watson, WCNC-Charlotte

IRE EXECUTIVE STAFF

Mark Horvit . . . . Executive Director
CONTACT INFORMATION

IRE and NICAR Database Library 573-884-7711
IRE Resource Center 573-882-3364
Membership Services 573-882-2042
                                                          or info@ire.org